Hollywood's Fallen Idols

Hollywood's Fallen Idols

ROY PICKARD

B.T. Batsford Ltd · London

First published 1989
© Roy Pickard 1989
ISBN 0 7134 6152 7

Typeset by Lasertext Limited,
Thomas Street, Stretford,
Manchester M32 0JT.
Printed in Great Britain by
Bath Press, Bath, Avon
for the publishers
B.T. Batsford Limited,
4 Fitzhardinge Street,
London W1H 0AH

*The photos on the cover show on the front
(clockwise from top right), Charlie Chaplin,
Marilyn Monroe, Montgomery Clift, George
Sanders and Judy Garland; and on the back,
Errol Flynn. (National Film Archive)*

Contents

Acknowledgements

The pictures in this book were originally used to publicize or promote films made or distributed by the following companies, to whom I gratefully offer acknowledgement:

Allied Artists, Avco-Embassy, Cannon-Classic, Cinerama, Columbia, Goldwyn, Lorimar, Metro-Goldwyn-Mayer, National Film Archive, Orion, Palace Pictures, Paramount, PRC, The Rank Organization, Republic, RKO/RKO Radio, Selznick, 20th Century Fox, UPI, United Artists, Universal/Universal-International, Virgin Films, Warner Brothers.

Errol Flynn in The Dawn Patrol, *1938.*

Introduction

Most of the stars discussed in this book could each be justifiably termed a 'Hollywood Great'. What makes them different from the Bogarts, the Gables, Hepburns, Cagneys and the rest is that, although each tasted success not one managed to hold onto it. For them stardom turned sour. Their tragedy (and each life included in this book is indeed a kind of tragedy) is that they failed to cope with the strains of their public lives and the relentless pressure put on them by the Hollywood studios. Sometimes it was their own self-destructive nature that caused their breakdown, often it was alcohol or drugs. But all had one thing in common; they fed off and eventually died because of their fame.

In focusing on these lives I have tried to view the stars compassionately and examine the reasons for their decline objectively; whether, for instance, their suffering was of their own making or whether the times in which they lived were responsible. Strangely, not one of the ten stars declined for the same reason. With Charlie Chaplin it was mainly his political problems that brought about his downfall, with Errol Flynn it was a frustrated need to be taken seriously, with Orson Welles the inability to meet the Hollywood machine on its own terms, with von Stroheim it was sheer extravagance. But whatever the reason, all tasted failure and rejection *after* their successes, not before, and this made their fate that much more difficult to take. Lesser stars often managed to bounce back, at least to a halfway success. Not, sadly, those included in these pages.

None of the chapters is meant to represent a life career even though they all take in various aspects of those careers. Rather, they are designed to focus on and isolate the turning points. The focus is thus on moments in time and how these moments led to fatal disintegration.

Numerous books and magazines and newspaper features have provided me with material for *Hollywood's Fallen Idols*, plus many of my own interviews in London and during three visits to Hollywood. I remember especially, and with pleasure, conversations with James Mason, Joseph Cotten, Van Johnson, Sterling Hayden, Charlton Heston, Vincente Minnelli, Edward Dmytryk, Shelley Winters, Bette Davis, Elia Kazan, Charles Walters, George Sidney, Richard Zanuck and David Brown, Robert Wise, Saul Chaplin and many others about the careers of the ten personalities I have included in this book.

The book is set mainly in what is termed Hollywood's Golden Age even though it does encroach into the 1960s and the 1970s. Whether things would be any different today had the stars lived in the modern era is difficult to say. Possibly, but not necessarily. The death of John Belushi and the faltering career of director Michael Cimino after *Heaven's Gate*, indicate that it can be just as difficult working in today's cinema.

Most of the stars here were hero-worshipped in their time; they represented the pinnacle of popular culture. Yet they were also victims of exploitation, even fatalists, who somehow seemed to sense that Hollywood would not be their salvation but would eventually destroy them. And if it didn't destroy them unaided, they themselves went out of their way to make sure that it did. This is how it happened . . .

1. Charlie Chaplin

Charlie Chaplin

The man behind the tramp. Charlie Chaplin, as he appeared without his famous tramp costume in Hollywood in the early 1920s.

Shortly after Charlie Chaplin died a newspaper reviewer suggested the following epitaph: 'Here lies Charles Spencer Chaplin who made more people laugh than any other human being in the history of the world.' Today, even though Chaplin's unique brand of silent pantomime holds less appeal than it used to, that epitaph still holds true. Thanks to the bowler hat, the tight-fitting jacket, the baggy trousers and the large boots, plus of course the cane and the funny walk, Chaplin remains a screen immortal.

Yet, back in the 1920s and 1930s, there were those living in Hollywood (most of them politically to the right of Attila The Hun) who regarded Chaplin with much less affection than the audiences who marvelled at his antics on screen across the world. Reactionary, patriotic forces and religious groups considered him arrogant and self important. They disliked his yearnings for intellectual respectability and his habit of lecturing on subjects about which he knew little but was prepared to give uninformed opinions. They were openly hostile to his left-wing sympathies and drew vicious parallels between what he said and how he lived – in millionaire luxury, yachting, partying and socializing with the élite of the day. And they had little time for his morals and his undisguised liking for young actresses, especially those in their teens. They also took exception to the fact that he had never taken out American citizenship. They argued that without Hollywood Chaplin would not have become the star he was. Chaplin, for his part, retorted that Hollywood owed him rather more than he owed it; that his comic genius had helped make the name Hollywood synonymous with quality entertainment. Through his two-reelers and silent features he reached and appealed to more people than any other film performer in the world.

It was this undeniable position of power that allowed Chaplin to keep his enemies at bay in the silent days of the cinema. And as long as the cinema remained silent he could not be touched. A millionaire several times over, he was beholden to no one studio. He was his own one-man show, the sole creator of all his films. He would write, produce, direct, act in and compose the music for all of them. He did *what* he pleased *when* he pleased. No other artist in Hollywood enjoyed such luxury or freedom.

Memories of his humble beginnings in a Kennington slum remained with him always. His early poverty and loneliness were reflected in his films as he rose to prominence in the cinema. He escaped by creating a world of his own but through his genius and his unique ability to appeal to the man in the street, allowed millions to find solace in that world.

On screen he represented Mr Everyman, the indestructible underdog who, in the guise of a tramp, reacted against the pompous, the self-satisfied and the greedy. Always the tramp would be at odds with the bully, battling against authority and subconsciously awakening in audiences the thought that authority might in fact be overthrown, not only on screen but also in real life. It was an anarchic conception and one that frightened the Hollywood moguls. In his seemingly simple comedies Chaplin preached a kind of knockabout revolution.

▲ *Charlie Chaplin with the dog 'Mut' in his three-reeler* A Dog's Life, *written and directed by Chaplin for First National in 1918.*

▶ *The Tramp! The face of the world's most beloved comedy figure.*

▶ *The costume that became famous throughout the world and served Chaplin in over 75 films in 22 years before he set it aside after* Modern Times.

▼ *Charlie Chaplin, with Allan Garcia as the circus proprietor, in* The Circus *(1928).*

Charlie Chaplin

Charlie Chaplin and Paulette Goddard in Chaplin's last silent film, Modern Times *(1936).*

Ironically, the seeds of Chaplin's downfall were sown by Chaplin himself when in 1936 he released *Modern Times*, his brilliant satire of the machine age. In the last scene he walked off into the sunset, arm in arm with Paulette Goddard. It was the last occasion his little tramp appeared on film. Chaplin, having decided some ten years after *The Jazz Singer* to at last embrace the sound medium, concluded that his tramp and sound simply wouldn't mix. He put away the tramp costume that had served him for 22 years in some 75 films and looked ahead to what he hoped would be an equally successful 'second' career. Had he been able to gaze into a crystal ball and take note of the events that were to befall him in the 1940s and 1950s he might well have hesitated and clung on to his creation a little while longer. The tramp had brought him luck from the moment he first donned the costume back in 1914. Without him Chaplin's luck simply ran out.

The film that Chaplin selected to launch the second phase of his career was *The Great Dictator*. Chaplin had long been concerned with and disturbed by the political events in Europe (especially the horrors of the Spanish Civil War) and believed that through the film medium he could comment on and perhaps even influence in some small way, the political decisions that would be made in the future.

His picture was both a satirical comedy of Hitler's Germany and an exercise in propaganda. Chaplin played a dual role, an impoverished Jewish barber and a Hitler-like dictator Adenoid Hynkel who presides over the mythical kingdom of Tomania. Those close to Chaplin argued against the wisdom of the venture. In 1939 America was distinctly pro-fascist in many of its attitudes. A Gallup Poll taken at the outbreak of the Second World War revealed that 96% of those interviewed opposed America's entry into the war. Chaplin ignored the advice and after many months of preparation went ahead. Shooting took 127 days during the last months of 1939 and the early months of 1940. The budget was $2,000,000.

Chaplin was understandably nervous when *The Great Dictator* premiered in New York in October, 1940. He knew that for the first time in years he was out on a limb and wide open to all kinds of criticism. He was talking for the first time on screen, the subject matter of his film was controversial, his tramp had gone. All this was worry enough, but what concerned him most was that even though the war had been raging in Europe for over a year, America had still not entered the conflict. Neither had Hollywood been exactly anxious to jump on the anti-Fascist bandwagon. They had made only a handful of films, among them *The Mortal Storm* and *Confessions Of A Nazi Spy*, that had openly dared to criticize the Nazi regime.

He was thankful, therefore, to emerge with reviews which, although mixed, were more complimentary than negative. Most critics agreed that in its most inspired moments *The Great Dictator* showed Chaplin at his best, notably when, as Hynkel, he performs a ballet with the globe of the world. But there was also criticism. One reviewer suggested, with some validity, that the film was two or three years too late and that to make an attack on Hitler who was then storming his way across Europe was tantamount to locking the stable door after the horse had bolted. Another critic complained that presenting Hitler as a buffoon and his Nazi thugs as variations of the Keystone Kops was treating an appalling regime too flippantly. Much later Chaplin said: 'Had I known of the actual horrors of the German concentration camps, I could not have made *The Great Dictator*. I could not have made fun of the homicidal insanity of the Nazis.'

But it was the film's climax that surprised everyone and really got Chaplin into trouble. Speaking as Chaplin, but through the character of the barber, he spent six minutes talking directly to the camera and making a plea for a better world.

> The way of life can be free and beautiful, but we have lost the way. Greed has poisoned men's souls – has barricaded the world with hate – has goosestepped us into misery and bloodshed. We have developed speed, but we have shut ourselves

Charlie Chaplin as Adenoid Hynkel in The Great Dictator *(1940). The role was the first played by Chaplin since his abandonment of his little tramp figure in 1936.*

in. Machinery that gives abundance has left us in want. Our knowledge has made us cynical; our cleverness, hard and unkind. We think too much and feel too little. More than machinery we need humanity. More than cleverness we need kindness and gentleness. Without these qualities, life will be violent and all will be lost.

There was nothing wrong with these sentiments. Indeed, they seem even more relevant today than they did in 1940. It was just that they jarred at the end of a film. Audiences who had just enjoyed a satirical indictment of the perils of dictatorship were then given a sermon as a postscript.

Those involved in the making of *The Great Dictator* had urged Chaplin to refrain from adding the epilogue. One of the salesmen for the film said that if Chaplin did include it it would knock at least a million dollars off the picture's gross. An obstinate Chaplin, who could be ruthless when making a film, retorted that he didn't care if it knocked off five million dollars he was going ahead anyway.

The general consensus was that Chaplin made a mistake in trying to propagandize. His enemies on the far right seized their opportunity, arguing that the speech smacked of Communism. They also made the most of a speech (made much later in 1942) when he stood in for the American ambassador in San Francisco and called for a second front in Europe to help the Russians in their fight against Hitler. He said:

> I am not a Communist. I am a human being, and I think I know the reactions of human beings. The Communists are no different from anyone else; whether they lose an arm or a leg, they suffer as all of us do, and die as all of us die. And the Communist mother is the same as any other mother. When she receives the tragic news that her sons will not return, she weeps as other mothers weep. I do not have to be a Communist to know that. And at this moment Russian mothers are doing a lot of weeping and their sons a lot of dying.

All of which was very emotional stuff and delivered with such power that those in the audience could hardly fail to be moved. But taken with his equally strong message at the end of *The Great Dictator* it simply added to the suspicions of many Americans that Chaplin was indeed a Communist even though he preceeded every speech by denying it.

The thing that most angered people about *The Great Dictator* (and it angered both his friends and his enemies) was that instead of simply entertaining his audience Chaplin insisted on lecturing and haranguing them, setting himself up as a self-important moralizer. When they pointed out that he was a comedian and film-maker and not a politician an unrepentant Chaplin replied:

> I saw no reason not to do it. The audience had their laughs and the picture was fun. But then I wanted the audiences to listen. I did the picture for the Jews of the world. I wanted to see the return of decency and kindness. I'm just a human being who wants to see this country a real democracy, and freedom from this infernal regimentation which is crawling over the rest of the world.

But if Chaplin's enemies enjoyed making capital out of his political views in the 1940s it was nothing compared to the malicious fun they delighted in over his private life. Always a great womanizer (he was married four times, on each occasion to girls in their late teens) and no stranger to court rooms over the years, he found himself assailed on all sides, first on a charge of income tax evasion, then in a plagiarism suit and finally in a paternity suit brought by a young actress named Joan Barry.

Chaplin managed to deal with the income tax charge without too much trouble, proving to the embarrassment of the Income Tax Authorities that he had

▲ Hynkel, the Great Dictator (Charlie Chaplin), and his aide, have to endure the rantings of Napaloni, Dictator of Bacteria (Jack Oakie).

actually overpaid by $24,938. The plagiarism suit, alleging that Chaplin had stolen the idea for *The Great Dictator*, was settled out of court. The red-headed Miss Barry, however, proved to be a much thornier problem.

A screen-struck girl of 21 seeking fame in the movies she first arrived in Hollywood in 1940. She was not unlike thousands of other girls trying to make it to the top in the movie capital. She had little talent, was not over attractive and relied on luck as much as anything else to get by. Almost immediately she struck lucky. After working as a waitress she was picked by oil millionaire J. Paul Getty to form part of the female entourage accompanying him to Mexico for the inauguration of Avila Camacho. Getty couldn't get her into the movies but a young agent who was also on the trip could. Tim Durant who was an agent for Chaplin's company United Artists took her along to one of Chaplin's Sunday tennis parties. Barry, not unaware of Chaplin's reputation, seized her chance and made an instant play for the comedian. Chaplin, never one to resist the charms of young ladies, returned the compliment. The result was a screen test and a promise to groom her for a key role in what was to be his next film.

Nothing came of the film and after months of coaching nothing came of Miss Barry either. Chaplin quickly tired of her, reducing her salary from $75 to $25 a week. He indicated that he thought it best she forgot about a film career and returned home.

Joan Barry, however, was not to be cast aside so easily. There were rumours that while she was being 'groomed' for stardom she had undergone two abortions. When Chaplin tried to rid himself of her she simply refused to go. Sometimes she would get drunk and drive up to Chaplin's house in the early hours of the morning. Once she crashed a Cadillac in Chaplin's driveway. On another occasion, when Chaplin refused to open the door to her persistent knocking, she began smashing the windows of his house. Chaplin, aware by then that she was something of a hopeless case and frightened that her drunkenness would become public (and harm his studio) quickly paid off $5,000 of Barry's debts. He bought one-way tickets for her and her mother to return to New York. Barry accepted the tickets and was on her way by 5 October 1942.

Chaplin obviously hoped that was the end of the affair and in nine cases out of ten it would have been. Joan Barry, however, was a persistent girl. In December, just a few weeks after her departure, she was back, pestering Chaplin with telephone calls. When that got her nowhere she decided to confront Chaplin face to face. On the night of 23 December she used a ladder to break into Chaplin's house, produced a gun she had purchased in a pawn shop and threatened to kill them both. There are two versions of what happened next. One, probably the more reliable, was that Chaplin, embarrassed because his two sons were in the house, took the gun away from her, gave her a sedative and locked her in a room, giving her some money the next morning as he let her out of the house. The other version, and the one insisted on by Barry, was that Chaplin amused at the idea and the melodrama of the situation, decided that the best way out of things was to have his way with her once more which he supposedly did on a bearskin rug in front of a blazing fire.

But, whichever version was correct, Chaplin could still not rid himself of her attentions. No sooner had he paid her off than she was back again. Close to desperation Chaplin called in the police who gave her a 90-day suspended sentence and ordered her to leave town. In May 1943 she returned, only this time, as Chaplin quickly realized, the situation was more serious. Barry informed him that she was six months pregnant and asked him what he was going to do about it. When he told her 'nothing', because he was not the father of the child, she earned herself more publicity by getting herself arrested on a vagrancy charge, spending most of the time in hospital because of her condition.

On 4 June she announced to the press that she was pregnant and that Chaplin was the father of her unborn child. The press, sensing a scandal of major proportions and the biggest Hollywood publicity circus in years spread Chaplin's picture across the front pages of their newspapers. Chaplin knew that it would be cheaper not to fight the case and settle out of court but that would have been an admission of guilt and he determined to fight things through to the end.

Joan Barry gave birth to a daughter in October 1943 and the case was set for the following February. Before that Chaplin had to face another charge – an indictment by a Federal grand jury that he had violated the Mann Act, passed in 1910 and designed to combat commercial prostitution. Chaplin was accused of having feloniously caused Joan Barry to be transported from Los Angeles to the city of New York with the intent and purpose of engaging in illicit sex relations. Again Chaplin protested his innocence and had to suffer the indignity of being photographed (quite irregularly) whilst having his fingerprints taken during the preliminary hearings. The brilliance of lawyer Jerry Giesler, who acted for many well-known Hollywood stars got him off and Chaplin was found not guilty.

But that was to be Chaplin's only moment of relief. The Joan Barry case was still to be settled. Chaplin agreed to a blood test to prove that he was not the father of the newly born child. The blood test proved conclusively that he was not the father. Research showed that parents of blood type O (Chaplin) and A (Joan Barry) could not produce a child of blood type B as the baby proved to be. Yet even with this proof a supreme court judge decided to overrule the evidence commenting that, 'The ends of justice will best be served by a full and fair trial of the issues.'

After that there was no way that Chaplin was going to win. A Los Angeles attorney described the decision of the judge as 'a landmark in the miscarriage of justice'. Chaplin, who had not hired Giesler in the confident belief that the scientific evidence would exonerate him, found that his own counsel was no match for the barnstorming prosecuting attorney who made headlines by indulging in some of the most vitriolic abuse heard from a lawyer in an American courtroom. Ignoring the evidence of the blood tests he hammered away day after day referring to Chaplin as 'a lecherous hound' and 'a little runt of a Svengali'. At one stage in the proceedings he even asked the jury to stare hard at the child (then a baby of a few months) and Chaplin and note the facial resemblance.

At the final count Chaplin, to no-one's surprise, was found guilty by an eleven to one vote. He was ordered to make payments of $75 a week to the child Carol Ann, with increases to $100 dollars as her needs grew until she reached the age of twenty-one. Shortly thereafter Joan Barry and her mother disappeared from Chaplin's life for good.

The damage done to Chaplin by the trial was immeasurable. It brought him the worst publicity he had ever had to endure and damaged his already faltering reputation. In court he once stood and cried out desperately at the judge: 'Your honour, I have committed no crime. I'm only human. But this man is trying to make a monster out of me.'

If it was the intention of those in high places in right-wing America to rid themselves of Chaplin for good they were well pleased with themselves by 1945. Just ten years before Chaplin had reigned supreme as the comic genius of the American cinema. A decade later he was almost a broken man. However, he still had one string to his bow, his new film *Monsieur Verdoux* which he had somehow managed to make despite all the traumas of the Barry trial. It was unfortunate that it should prove to be even more controversial than *The Great Dictator*. The story of a French bluebeard who murders his wives for money, it offered a pacifist text that argued that if war was the natural extension of diplomacy then murder was the natural end result of big business. There were no signs of the tramp in *Monsieur Verdoux*. There had been an occasional similarity between the barber and the tramp in *The Great Dictator*. But there was none in the 1947 film. This was a new Chaplin, an ironical natty figure, polished and gentlemanly with a cut away coat and striped trousers.

The film divided the critics as Chaplin hoped it would. He was perfectly prepared to argue his case for the film at a press conference specially arranged just prior to its premiere. But no-one at the press conference was in the slightest bit interested in discussing the film. What they now wanted to know was whether Chaplin was or was not a Communist. The humiliation of the Barry case was now out of the way and it was time once more to concentrate on the political aspects of Chaplin's life. Chaplin protested that he had attended the conference to discuss the film. When he eventually bowed to their pressure and made the simple statement that he was 'a citizen of the world' all the old doubts were raised once more.

Monsieur Verdoux was Chaplin's first commercial failure. Over-literary and stagey, and with elaborate dialogue, it proved to be ahead of its time, illuminating the coming protest of the post-war generation about a world that makes heroes of the most able killers in wartime, and criminals of them in peacetime. It drew sign-carrying pickets instead of throngs of patrons and played in just 2075 theatres, earning a paltry $375,000. Joseph Vogel, the general manager of the Loew's chain of cinemas, said: 'It's amazing how little the Chaplin picture did... maybe what audiences wanted was the old clown.'

By some miracle Chaplin did not have to face the Un-American Activities Committee like so many others of the time. He was called but courageously refused, informing representative J. Parnell Thomas in a sarcastic telegram:

> You have been quoted as saying you wish to ask me if I am a Communist. You sojourned for ten days in Hollywood not long ago and could have asked me the question at that time, effecting something of an economy, or you could telephone me now – collect. In order that you may be completely up-to-date on my thinking I suggest you view carefully my latest production *Monsieur Verdoux*. It is against war and the futile slaughter of our youth. I trust you will not find its humane message distasteful. While you are preparing your engraved subpoena I will give you a hint on where I stand. I am not a Communist. I am a peacemonger.

Chaplin was subpoena'd three times to appear before the House Un-American Activites Committee but each time the date was postponed. Finally, a telegram arrived saying that he would not, after all, be needed. Perhaps those in court felt that Chaplin might steal the show and upstage them and they may well have been right in this assumption. Many years later Chaplin stated that if he had have

▶ *Two of the world's greatest entertainers: Chaplin with Al Jolson just prior to the première of Chaplin's 1947 film,* Monsieur Verdoux.

▽ *Charlie Chaplin as the faded music hall comedian Calvero and his young protegée, ballerina Claire Bloom, in* Limelight *(1952).*

been called he would have appeared as the tramp, complete with baggy pants, bowler and cane. Those attacking Chaplin in the Barry paternity suit may well have felt that they had the little man on the run; Chaplin in tramp costume mocking his inquisitors would have been a different story altogether.

There were those who attacked him though – and with some force. Journalist Westbrook Pegler devoted a whole column to abusing him in December 1947. He referred to Chaplin as 'an alien, guilty of moral turpitude which disqualifies him from citizenship. Caught in the act of cheating the government of an enormous debt for taxes, he was a slacker in both World Wars, although he clamoured with the Communists for a second front in the latest one.' The same year a US Congressman, John E. Rankin, demanded his deportation, asserting that the film actor's life was 'detrimental to the moral fabric of America'. By deporting him, 'he can be kept off the screen and his loathsome pictures can be kept from the eyes of American youth.'

In the end Hollywood did manage to 'get' Chaplin. It had taken them more than 30 years but they finally found the 'evidence' they needed to rid themselves of him once and for all. Or at least the authorities claimed they did. Their chance occurred when Chaplin decided to hold the premiere of his last American film *Limelight* in Britain rather than the States. The film was the story of a fading music hall comedian who helps a young ballerina (played by newcomer Claire Bloom) to become a star. Buster Keaton featured in a few memorable moments with Chaplin and the picture, in which Chaplin poured memories of his London boyhood, was more warmly received than *Monsieur Verdoux*.

While he was on board the Queen Elizabeth and heading for England the American Attorney General James McGranery rescinded Chaplin's re-entry permit and ordered the Immigration and Naturalization Service to hold him for hearings when – or if – he attempted to re-enter the country. Just why was never revealed. McGranery said: 'If what has been said about Chaplin is true he is, in my opinion, an unsavoury character.' But that was all. There were only hints that so-called evidence had been found. Later it was learned that J. Edgar Hoover and the FBI had been compiling a 900-page dossier on him for some 50 years and had even sought scientific advice on how he might be framed in the Joan Barry case when the blood tests proved to be in his favour. That Chaplin survived in Hollywood as long as he did was something of a minor miracle.

On his arrival in London Chaplin protested his innocence, but those close to him thought his protests half-hearted. He had tired of all his problems in America and just prior to his departure had told a friend that he had a premonition that he would not be returning. And so it proved. He withdrew his assets from America and headed for Switzerland where he lived happily with his wife Oona (whom he had married in 1943 and who had borne him eight children) until his death, aged 88, on Christmas Day 1977.

He fell from favour during his retirement. Audiences no longer found his clown as appealing as they once had. Critics showed a distinct preference for Buster Keaton's abilities. But Keaton himself said: 'At his best, and Chaplin

Calvero — Chaplin's last performance in an American film — and in this still at least, still showing shades of the little tramp!

remained at his best for a long time, he was the greatest comedian who ever lived.' George Bernard Shaw referred to him as 'the only genius ever developed in motion pictures'. Charles Laughton, when asked to recall the three greatest performances he had ever seen on the screen, said all of them would be by Chaplin!

In his final years he journeyed twice to England, first in the late 1950s to make the comedy *A King In New York* and then again in the mid-1960s to make the romantic comedy *A Countess From Hong Kong* with Marlon Brando and Sophia Loren. Both were failures which distressed him, especially as the critics accused him of being old-fashioned and no longer in touch with what the public wanted in the way of entertainment. He said:

> What do they want from me? The sexy, violent muck which fouls up the screen today? I saw a film privately the other night which reduced human love to the level of the farmyard. Don't people believe in tenderness any more — the magic that comes with the mere squeezing of a hand.

Chaplin with his wife Oona during their visit to Britain to make A Countess from Hong Kong *(1967).*

His final years, the last 25, were happy ones. They allowed him to forget, but only partially, how he had been treated in the country that had been his home for so many years. He did make one final visit there in April 1972 when he was honoured with a special Academy Award for 'the sum of his screen achievements through more than 50 years'. He had only ever received one Oscar, back in 1929 when he earned a special award for *The Circus*. The 1972 honorary award was presented by Jack Lemmon. Chaplin wandered onto the stage not quite knowing where he was and almost unable to speak. 'Thank you', he said at last. 'Words seem, oh so futile, so feeble. This is a very emotional moment for me.' Jack Lemmon, tears in his eyes, stepped forward and handed Chaplin the bowler and cane. Chaplin just stood there alone in front of the 3000 strong audience. That audience rose giving him a standing ovation that lasted for several minutes. Very few in the audience that night had had anything to do with the vitriolic attacks made on Chaplin in the 1940s but even though they stood applauding and cheering there was still the sense that in a way the reconciliation was somehow phoney; a public apology for the benefit of the world's press. It didn't quite work. It looked and sounded like a staged event. In reality Chaplin and Hollywood were still miles apart. And they had been that way ever since the famous costume had been put away in mothballs all those years before, when Chaplin and Goddard had walked off into that sunset. What came afterwards was vilification, abuse and a vicious hounding that belongs in the worst chapters of Hollywood history. Chaplin at least survived the ordeal which is probably more than his persecutors in Hollywood would have wished.

2. *Montgomery Clift*

Montgomery Clift

On the evening of 12 May 1956 Montgomery Clift changed his mind and went to a party. He did so against his better judgement. Tired and bored and depressed about the film he was making, he had decided to watch some TV and go to bed early. But the telephone kept ringing and every time it was Elizabeth Taylor at the end of the line. She was giving a small dinner party that night and wanted Monty to come. He refused, excusing himself because he was exhausted and did not trust himself behind the wheel of his car anymore. She persisted. So too did her then husband Michael Wilding. Eventually Clift relented and at seven that evening drove slowly up to Liz Taylor's house, just five minutes away in the Benedict Canyon Hills.

The evening was a tame affair. Rock Hudson was there with his secretary Phyllis Gates; so too were actor Kevin McCarthy, Michael Wilding, who was in pain with a bad back, and Liz who entertained herself mainly by listening to Nat King Cole and Frank Sinatra records. Clift drank a few half-glasses of wine and excused himself early. He asked McCarthy, a longtime friend, if he would drive ahead of him down the canyon. He hadn't driven for months and was a little unsure of himself on the narrow, twisting roads.

McCarthy drove slowly at first but then accelerated when he glanced in his rearview mirror and saw Clift's car close behind him. The lights of Clift's car suddenly began to weave from one side of the road to the other and McCarthy wondered if Clift was having a blackout. As he negotiated one of the bends he heard a loud crash. He stopped and ran back. Clift's car was crushed against a telephone pole. It was dark. McCarthy couldn't see Clift but he could smell petrol. He managed to turn off the ignition and then drove back to Taylor's house. He pounded on the door, yelling 'Monty's had a terrible accident. I don't know whether he's alive. Get an ambulance quick!'

Elizabeth Taylor was the first to reach Monty's wrecked car. Unable to open the front door she forced open the back and crawled over the seat. Crouching down, she gently put Clift's head in her lap. Blood was gushing from his face. He moaned, pointed to his mouth and started to choke. She forced open his mouth and, plunging her hand down his throat, pulled out two teeth that had lodged in his windpipe.

It took Rock Hudson and the doctor nearly half an hour to ease Clift from the wrecked car. When they reached the Cedars Of Lebanon Hospital, Elizabeth Taylor, her dress smeared with dried blood, at last broke down. She said later: 'When they wheeled him into the operating theatre Monty's head was so swollen it was almost as wide as his shoulders. His eyes had disappeared. His cheeks were level with his nose.'

Apart from suffering from whiplash, Clift's injuries were entirely facial. He had heavy lacerations down the left side of his face. There were numerous cuts under his eyes. His nose was broken. So too was his sinus cavity. His jaw was crushed on both sides and smashed in four separate places. One whole cheekbone was cracked. Several teeth were missing. He was also suffering from cerebral concussion.

The doctors did their best to maintain Clift's appearance even though they decided against plastic surgery. Clift's jaw remained wired for nine weeks. A slight scar on the bridge of his nose and his torn upper lip brought about the most pronounced change to his looks. There was also a slight thickening of his facial characteristics and an immobility in the left side of his face, caused by severed nerves. He was still only 36 but looked considerably older. In the film he was making at the time of the accident – the epic *Raintree County* – he was supposed to be a man in his twenties.

MGM had been shooting *Raintree County* for six weeks when the accident occurred which meant they were were not even halfway through the schedule. There were still many weeks of filming left and Clift was in almost every scene. Clift, anxious not to let anyone down and not because he held any great love for the picture, announced that he would carry on. His friends tried to argue him out of it. Even before filming had begun Clift's health had been in a fragile condition. To resume the film at such short notice would simply ruin his health still further. For their part MGM were only too anxious for Clift to continue. They had five million dollars tied up in the production and the delay had already cost them another two million. Premiere dates had been booked and release dates mapped out for the film's roadshow engagements in 1957. To have delayed the release of *Raintree County* would have hurt the studio considerably for the film was being photographed in the new wide-screen process 'Camera 65' and needed special handling.

Studio head Dore Schary realized that starting the picture again without Clift might also present them with trouble from Elizabeth Taylor. He said:

> After we learned the extent of Monty's injuries there was some talk at the studio suggesting that we recast his role, take our insurance funds and redo what we had already photographed. My own views were that we were rushing a decision prematurely; that if Monty recovered and I had summarily booted him out of the picture we would have done him an injustice. Also I felt sure that Elizabeth Taylor, who adored Monty, would refuse to do the film and be willing to face suspension. I talked to her and she confirmed my opinions. We closed down the company and waited for Monty to recover.

That Clift should suffer such an accident whilst making a film of the 'quality' of *Raintree County* was a supreme irony. It wasn't his kind of film at all, just a love story between an idealistic Yankee schoolteacher and a predatory Southern belle during the American Civil War. MGM advertised it as another *Gone With The Wind*. Clift preferred to call it 'soap opera with elephantitis'. The main reason he had agreed to make it was because he would be teamed once more with Elizabeth Taylor with whom he had last worked five years earlier in the classic *A Place In The Sun*. He was also broke. Before he began work on *Raintree County* he hadn't made a movie for two and half years. During that time he had turned down 163 scripts and managed to survive only by borrowing heavily from his agents at MCA. By early 1956 he was deeply in debt. He thus found himself in the

Wayne versus Clift – and losing! A scene from Montgomery Clift's first movie: the Howard Hawks Western Red River *(1948).*

position he had always dreaded; for the first time he was making a film simply for the money. Hollywood had always depressed him and whenever he was required to stay there for any length of time he would invariably finish his letters to his friends with two words – 'Vomit, California.' Now, with *Raintree County*, his sellout seemed complete. Even when he told MGM to reduce his $300,000 salary by $50,000 and use the money to improve the film's script, it didn't help. He felt trapped.

Ten years earlier things had been very different. Slender, darkly handsome and with large haunted eyes he seemed a natural for stardom. Just about all the major studios tried to sign him even though his first screen test, for the Robert Mitchum western *Pursued*, had been a failure. Metro had seen his potential as early as 1941 when they offered him a role in their classic tearjerker *Mrs. Miniver*.

Clift turned everything down, signing only a one picture deal with Howard

▼ *Montgomery Clift and Joanne Dru in* Red River.

Hawks to appear in the John Wayne western *Red River*. He had always been attracted by movies and Hollywood but was only too well aware of what had happened to other young hopeful stage actors. The thought that he too might finish up a failure and disillusioned at an early age made him tread warily. But, perhaps what worried him even more than failure was the possibility that he might become a commodity first, a star second and an actor third.

He didn't like his performance in *Red River*. He called it 'mediocre'. Neither did he get on particularly well with Hawks, or his co-star John Wayne and his macho cronies. On location in Arizona he felt as though he were in a foreign land. But when he first caught a glimpse of himself on screen he realized there was no going back. Later, when he was working on *From Here To Eternity*, he told author James Jones: 'I watched myself in *Red River* and I knew I was going to be famous. So I decided I would get drunk anonymously for one last time.'

The idea of losing his privacy terrified Clift. What spurred him on was the thought that, if he was lucky, film-making could be an intelligent, fulfilling and constructive experience. Directors such as Fred Zinnemann (for whom he made *The Search* and *From Here To Eternity*) and George Stevens (*A Place In The Sun*) convinced him that he could become the finest of all the post-war American actors, better even than Brando.

And at the beginning of his career most of Hollywood's top directors seemed to agree. Not only Zinnemann and Stevens but also Wyler (for whom Clift played the unscrupulous fortune hunter, Morris Townsend in *The Heiress*), Hitchcock and Billy Wilder stood in line for his services, although the latter was none too pleased when Clift withdrew from *Sunset Boulevard* just two weeks before that film started production.

Directors found in Clift an actor with all the qualities of the sensitive outsider, a victim, vulnerable and haunted, a man unable to escape his own destiny. He was the first of the rebel stars. Brando was lower class and brutish, all snarl and grunt, Dean was the defenceless neurotic. Clift was the upper-class rebel, quiet and intelligent and thoughtful but still a rebel. On screen he was usually the loner battling against the odds and generally losing; the young factory worker driven to murder because of an impossible love in *A Place In The Sun*; the stubborn individualist Prewitt at odds with the army in *From Here to Eternity*; the young priest tortured by his vow of silence in Hitchcock's *I Confess*. In the 1950s younger audiences closely identified with loners. Clift was the most sensitive of them all. His inwardness gave an incredible intensity to his acting.

Opinions of his talent were mostly favourable even though John Wayne called him an 'arrogant little bastard'. Spencer Tracy said of him: 'He makes most of today's young players look like bums' Fred Zinnemann called him a 'great actor' and Edward Dmytryk who directed him in *Raintree County* and *The Young Lions* said: 'He was an exceptionally bright young man who liked to pretend he wasn't, unlike Brando who likes to pretend he's bright, whereas in fact, he isn't very.' Dmytryk added: 'I enjoyed working with Monty more than any other actor in my experience. He never hurt anyone except himself. He was intelligent, thoughtful, humorous and caring. He was a man with no skin – all his nerve ends were exposed'

When Clift eventually decided to stay in Hollywood (he signed a three-picture deal with Paramount in the late 1940s) it soon became apparent that none of the studio publicity machines knew what to do with him. He was not interested in making an impression. He wasn't after stardom. He didn't want a seven-year contract. All he wanted to do was to act. In this respect he was like Brando. Together they were totally unconcerned with image; both were forerunners of the stars who came later in the 1970s and 1980s.

Clift's unorthodox attitudes towards Hollywood naturally intrigued the fan magazines. Shortly after his early film successes he was photographed having dinner at a Hamburger Heaven counter. He was also pictured listening dreamily to classical music. He was even shown reading a book. Hollywood reporters,

▲ *Montgomery Clift and the Oscar-winning Olivia de Havilland in William Wyler's* The Heiress *(1949).*

▶ *Montgomery Clift and Paul Douglas in* The Big Lift *(1950), one of Clift's lesser known films, made at the time of the Berlin air lift.*

Arguably Clift's finest role: as the doomed George Eastman in George Steven's masterpiece, A Place in the Sun *(1951). Sharing the scene; Elizabeth Taylor, who made three films with the actor.*

desperate to conjure up some sort of image for him, found themselves coming up with a lot of negatives: Clift did not go to parties, he did not chase starlets or indulge in fake romances, he was not interested in food and he dressed like a man who was on the unemployment line. None of which interested Clift in the least. He said: 'I am neither a young rebel nor a tired rebel but quite simply an actor who is trying to do his job with the maximum of conviction and sincerity.'

He enlarged on his acting philosophy when he said:

I'm not afraid of being typed. The big danger is playing safe. The strongest motivating force in an actor is experimentation. Anything that stretches you is worth playing, even if it's a flop.

In many respects, the screen is a more satisfying medium than the stage. Sincerity comes across better, and there is more chance for subtlety because the camera is on you all the time.

When the studio heads told him that his independence might not be all he hoped for and that he would make mistakes, Clift retorted: 'You don't understand. I want to be free to do so.'

In his private life Clift was very much like the characters he played on screen, a tortured man who at the age of thirty was insecure, full of anxieties about his career and already a hardened drinker. In 1950 he was persuaded to attend some Alcoholic Anonymous meetings but the AA failed to cure him. The same year he was admitted to the Neurological Centre at Columbia Presbyterian Hospital and was detoxified. He worried too about his inability to maintain a long and meaningful relationship. He found it difficult to accept that he was bisexual. He said: 'I have my deepest relationships with women yet it is with men that I find more satisfaction in bed.' He was also extremely careless about his relationships. Never once did he stop to consider that he was a major Hollywood actor and that the press were always lying in wait. His lawyer managed to quash a story about Monty and a young man he had tried to solicit on 42nd Street. There were many other such casual pickups that, luckily, did not reach the attentions of the press.

Elizabeth Taylor was the woman with whom he enjoyed the longest relationship. They met and fell in love whilst filming *A Place In The Sun*, an adaptation of Theodore Dreiser's novel *An American Tragedy*. Their affair was never consummated but lasted on and off for many years. George Stevens used gigantic close-ups for their love scenes in *A Place In The Sun* and the effect was mesmerizing.

The fact that he was working with directors of the calibre of Stevens and Zinnemann should have quelled any doubts Clift may have had about his status in Hollywood but his self-destructive nature kept gnawing away at him. At the back of his mind was the fear that he was really kidding himself and that he was involved in a lost cause. He seemed almost to will himself into failure. After a disastrous attempt to make a film in Italy with Vittorio De Sica, *Indiscretion Of*

Montgomery Clift on trial in his only Hitchcock film, !
Confess (1953), the story of a priest whose vows prevent him from revealing the identity of a murderer.

Clift, with Frank Sinatra, in Fred Zinnemann's From Here to Eternity *(1953).*

An American Wife starring Jennifer Jones, he rejected everything that came his way. He turned down the Paul Newman part in *Cat On A Hot Tin Roof*, he said no to the Brando role in *On The Waterfront* and to James Dean's tormented hero in *East Of Eden*. He also refused the opportunity to play Ishmael in Huston's *Moby Dick. War And Peace, Sons And Lovers* and Wyler's *Friendly Persuasion* were other films he declined.

Bill Gunn, a black actor who knew him in the 1950s, said: 'He should not have been so choosy. If he had found a role that half suited him rather than settling for his idea of perfection his life might not have turned in on itself.'

That he might make a bad film or even fail in a picture that he believed in did not worry Clift unduly; that he would give an inferior performance in a film he knew was going to be second-rate before he stepped in front of the cameras depressed him. That is why *Raintree County* had such a devastating effect on him, not just because of the accident but because he was suddenly something he had never wanted to be – a commercial property.

His friends were convinced that he went back to work too early on *Raintree County*. He was in great pain and under medication as he felt the pressure to 'keep up' with the schedule. His face was still swollen but his right profile was the least damaged so director Edward Dmytryk filmed him from that angle as much as possible. Twice he was found wandering naked at night in the streets of Natchez. He drank and found solace in drugs. He carried with him a black satchel in which he kept over 200 kinds of pills – barbiturates, tranquillizers, painkillers, something for every emergency.
Edward Dmytryk recalled:

> Monty was damaged psychologically. He fell apart after we resumed production and became less and less responsible as the picture progressed, but this could have been due to any one of a dozen reasons. Checking his behaviour out with some of his friends. I learned that he had been prone to such periods of instability at various times long before the accident. Clift was a very complicated man, and the behaviour he exhibited over the ensuing months stemmed from causes far deeper than the simple trauma of an accident.

Dore Schary said:

> When he checked back in after a long, painful healing process, we had to face the sad fact that Monty was hooked on drugs and liquor that eased his pain and drove the demons from his mind.
>
> Elizabeth was totally supportive. She nursed him, aided and covered for him. On the very bad days she called me for help, and during the time we continued our production I became fond of Monty. There was a little boy vulnerability about him; beneath the pain, drugs and liquor there was a generous and dear young man who had not matured emotionally. It was as if a fourteen-year-old had suddenly moved into a thirty-year-old time frame and that, coupled with the accident, seemed to doom him. He exaggerated the extent of his disfigurement and rushed into the comforting arms of pills and alcohol.

▲ *Marlon Brando (left) visiting director Fred Zinnemann and Montgomery Clift on the set of* From Here to Eternity.

▶ *Montgomery Clift with Jennifer Jones in De Sica's* Indiscretion of an American Wife, *(1954).*

◀ *Montgomery Clift as Private Prewitt, in* From Here to Eternity, *who refuses to box in his regimental team because he once blinded a man in the ring.*

In November 1956 Marlon Brando, concerned about reports of Monty trying to destroy himself through the lethal combination of pills and booze, paid a visit to Clift in New York in the hope that he could persuade him to calm down. There had always been a friendly rivalry between the two – both had been referred to as the finest actor to emerge on post-war American screens – and Brando was anxious for the competition between them to continue. He told Clift that he would stand no chance if he wrecked himself physically. Clift was genuinely touched by Brando's concern but ignored his advice. When Brando offered to help 'dry him out' he turned that down too. And all the time he was refusing Brando's help he was downing double vodkas.

Raintree County made money but it was not the critical success everyone at MGM had hoped for. It was dull, long, flat and boring. It lasted for three hours and during that time nothing much happened. The public were shocked by the new look Clift, who summed up the picture thus:

> The actors and Edward Dmytryk tried to lift its lousy script from the soap opera level. But we couldn't raise it more than a couple of inches which was far from getting it to the realm of merit. Another unfortunate thing about the movie was that the audience spent too much trying to figure out which scenes were *after* my accident. Imagine charging 16 dollars for four people to see *Raintree County* which is what some friends of mine had to pay because it was being road-shown on a two-a-day basis.

Clift worked again with Dmytryk after *Raintree County* on a disappointing version of Irwin Shaw's fine war novel *The Young Lions*. He also appeared in an adaptation of Nathaniel West's *Lonelyhearts* (as an idealistic reporter victimized by his own conscience) and in Stanley Kramer's *Judgement At Nuremberg* in which he looked 10 sometimes 20 years older than his 40 years. He played a feeble-minded baker's assistant whom the Nazis have sterilized. He worked for only two days on the picture and did the part for nothing. When his agent demanded his usual high fee he sent the agent an empty paper bag containing his commission. Stanley Kramer said:

> Clift was a really wonderful actor. But he needed somebody to be terribly kind, somebody who would say, 'You're wonderful and I know that you're having a little trouble and you don't remember the lines, but what's the difference? Within the scope of the thing, you just do it as you feel it should be, and we'll manage it. But Monty, you're wonderful and I wanted you for the part, etc., etc.' I had to bolster his confidence all the time.
>
> It was really Spencer Tracy who pulled him through in that film. Monty was literally going to pieces. Tracy just grabbed his shoulders and told him he was the greatest young actor of his time and to look deep into his eyes and play to him and the hell with the lines. And it worked.

During the last six years of his life Clift became increasingly difficult to work with. His nerves were in shreds, he behaved boorishly and was sometimes maniacal and unpredictable in his moods. Totally unable to control his drinking or his drug taking he became known in the industry as 'a risk'.

Elia Kazan, who had directed him in *The Skin Of Our Teeth* on Broadway sixteen years earlier, worked with him for the first time on film when he came to make *Wild River* in 1960. Clift played a TVA administrator who tries to persuade an elderly matriarch (played by Jo Van Fleet) to sell her property so that it can be inundated as part of the TVA's dam network. Kazan said:

> He was no longer handsome, and there was a strain everywhere in him − even it seemed, in his effort to stand erect.
>
> I also had to cope with the problem about which everyone had warned me. Monty's drinking. Before agreeing to take him for the part I'd extracted a solemn promise that he would not take a drink from the first day of work until the last. He kept his promise, surviving days of stress and physical discomfort without the help of a bottle until the very last day, when he arrived on the set swaying on his feet, then keeled over. When I got to him on the ground, he was asleep. I forgave him the lapse; I thought he'd done well by me. I knew I was handling a sick man, who was good-hearted and in no way evil. I can still recall the pathetic happy laugh that would burst out of him, then subside just as suddenly. I knew that each morning he underwent the humiliation of covering the transparent areas in his thinning hair with black make-up. As we went along, his confidence grew. Despite all, I felt tender towards him. He was just a boy.

Joseph Mankiewicz was another director who took a risk with Clift when he filmed Tennessee Williams', steamy play *Suddenly Last Summer*. Clift played a doctor brought in by an ageing widow (Katharine Hepburn) to perform a lobotomy on her niece who is incarcerated in a crumbling asylum in the Deep

South. The film was morbid, talky stuff. Homosexuality, madness and cannibalism were among its ingredients. The niece was played by Elizabeth Taylor (her third film with Clift); Mercedes McCambridge featured as her mother. McCambridge said:

> Everyone connected with the film was so unhappy. The ambience and the vibrations were upsetting. I'm glad I wasn't in it more than I was. I was bitterly unhappy. Elizabeth was still mourning Mike Todd. Miss Hepburn was suffering through Spencer Tracy's illness. Joe had something wrong with his hands – a skin disease – and he had to wear gloves all the way through the picture. I don't think you would think of Gore Vidal or Tennessee Williams as particularly happy people. Of course Monty was in torment. Everyone connected with the film was going through some kind of personal anguish and showed it.

Clift found it difficult to remember his lines. He had one scene in which he was supposed to perform a delicate brain operation in front of students. He had to deliver half a page of dialogue in one take but found the task too much. He kept blowing. Finally Mankiewicz broke the scene down into 14 separate takes, one line per take. For Clift it was humiliating, for Mankiewicz the ultimate professional it was exasperating. He asked producer Sam Spiegel if Clift could be replaced. Spiegel said:

> We were frequently tempted because it became increasingly more difficult to work with him on certain days. And then there were days when he was considerably more relaxed. I was very fond of him ... I spent hours and hours during the picture practically nursing him – postponing the shooting until I knew that he was calm and that we had given him enough coffee and enough counter-medicines to counteract whatever drugs he was taking.

Mercedes McCambridge's memory of Clift was of a sad, almost hopeless individual, fighting the heat of an English summer and the effects of the DTs.

> I can see him now with his shoulder blades hunched and pinched in that way of his. It wasn't that he was round-shouldered; it was as if, no matter how loose he seemed in the rest of his body, there was always that terrible tension. He was dripping wet all of the time. I can remember mopping his brow several times trying hard not to spoil his makeup. Once in a while, I would go over to him and stand behind his chair and put my hands on his shoulders and keep them there for a while. My heart ached for him.

John Huston, who had earlier worked successfully with Clift on *The Misfits* found he experienced as much frustration as Joe Mankiewicz when he cast Clift as *Freud* in 1962. Again Clift had trouble with his lines and again he found himself working with a director who wasn't wholly sympathetic to his personal problems. Huston had had enough trouble with the film's script and getting the project off the ground to worry too much about his actors. The delays to filming were costly. At one stage, Clift, worried because of his apparently failing eyesight, flew from the Vienna locations to London to see a specialist. He eventually had an operation for the removal of cataracts in both eyes. Universal sued Clift for nearly $700,000 because of the delays in filming, caused mainly by his leaving the

Clift as Rudolf Peterson, a pathetic, emasculated victim of Nazi surgery in Stanley Kramer's Judgment at Nuremberg *(1961).*

set and refusing to learn his lines. Clift later told his brother: 'I can remember lines in one second if they're valid. I can't memorize a line that I don't believe.' Universal finished owing Clift $131,000 in overtime. They refused to pay until their own suit was cleared up. Clift lodged a countersuit claiming that the film's delays were caused by the rewriting of the screenplay. In 1963 the suit was settled – in Clift's favour.

The real loser on the film was John Huston. *Freud* had long been a pet project of his and had taken him years to get off the ground. There was little pleasure to be enjoyed during the filming. He said:

> Monty was supposedly on the wagon, so no one ever saw him with a drink in his hand, but I soon discovered that each time he passed the bar he'd pick up a bottle or whatever was handy, tip it up and drink from the bottle directly, then wander off.
>
> Monty also wanted to sit in on our discussions about the script. He had been seeing psychiatrists since 1950 and fancied himself an expert on Freud. Monty would come into the room, take off his shoes and lie down on the floor. He said it was the only way he could think. He would interrupt at the wrong moments, and his remarks were largely incomprehensible. His presence served only to delay and confuse. One day I told him we couldn't include him anymore, explained why, and shut and locked the door. Monty stood outside the door and cried. Then he turned to the bar and drank himself unconscious.
>
> Monty's dialogue in the film would have taxed the technique of a fine actor at his best; and Monty was far from being at his best. His accident some years before had done him great damage. There had been head injuries and there is no doubt in my mind that they included brain damage. His prior brilliance now came through in fitful flashes. His petulant and obstinate behaviour was an attempt to hide from me and the others – and probably himself – that he was no longer able to contend. I'm sure Monty had almost no conception of the significance of what he said in the picture – yet he had the ability to make you believe that he did. There was a mist between him and the rest of the world that you simply couldn't penetrate. It must have been agony for him during those moments when he was fully aware. At times I saw a crucified look on his face.

When he died in his New York home from a heart attack on 23 July 1966 Montgomery Clift was just 45. He had made only one film since *Freud*, a spy thriller called *The Defector* which had still to be released. The major companies would no longer insure him. He was too much of a risk. Elizabeth Taylor was doing her best to interest Warner Bros in Clift for the lead in *Reflections In A Golden Eye*. But even she was having a hard time in convincing the studio that it would be worth their while. They could see – as indeed could everyone – that the Montgomery Clift that everyone remembered from just a decade earlier no longer existed. The dark, brooding eyes and haunted good looks had been replaced by a face that was ravaged beyond all recognition. He had varicose veins, suffered from a thyroid condition and his hands were gnarled from arthritis. It was difficult to come to terms with Elia Kazan's assertion that, during the 1940s, he had been 'the most beautiful man on the New York stage'.

There are those who say that Clift brought everything on himself and that no-one was really to blame. Marilyn Monroe once said: 'He's the only person I know who is in worse shape than I am'. Certainly no-one seems to know just how much the car accident was responsible for his subsequent decline. The directors who worked with him before that May date in 1956 – Wyler, Zinnemann, Stevens – never worked with him again. Those who filmed with him after the car crash – Huston, Dmytryk, Kazan – saw a very different actor

Two of the screen's losers! Monty Clift and Marilyn Monroe together for the first and only time in John Huston's The Misfits *(1961).*

from the one who enjoyed so much adulation at the beginning of his career.

Montgomery Clift remained an enigma right to the end. It's possible that he might have been spared some of his anguish if he had remained on stage and practised his craft on Broadway and in London. But as his private life seemed to spill over into so many of his performances anyway, that seems unlikely. Even a stage career would not have saved Montgomery Clift. He seemed to feel guilty about his success. More than anything he had a death wish. His final years have been described as the longest suicide in Hollywood history and, in retrospect that seems an accurate conclusion. He had all the talent, much more than most. He should have become and remained a major star but he went out of his way to wilfully prevent that stardom from happening.

3. Errol Flynn

Errol Flynn

A handsome, debonair cavalier; Errol Flynn, at the height of his Warner fame in the 1930s.

In the Raoul Walsh western *The Tall Men* Robert Ryan says of Clark Gable (who played a soldier of fortune in the film): 'He's what every boy wants to be when he grows up and what every man, looking back, wishes he had been'

Ryan was, of course, referring to a fictional character but he might just as well have been talking about the real-life Errol Flynn. In the 1930s and 1940s the boys who gazed in awe at Flynn's athletic screen exploits would undoubtedly have agreed with the accolade. So too, come to that, would many grown men, albeit for different reasons. During his peak years Errol Flynn, and his much publicized amorous, hard-drinking escapades, was the envy of most males who went to the movies regularly. It was only in Flynn's final years, as he approached an early death, that those same admiring men tended to revise their opinions. When they gazed at the weary, bloated, hollow-eyed features that stared back at them from the newspapers and remembered Flynn as he had been in his youth they felt that perhaps they were the ones who were better off. They could see all too clearly what a lifetime of highly charged living could do to the features of the human face. Flynn died when he was just fifty but into those fifty years he crammed more living than someone twice that age.

At the autopsy in Vancouver after his death of a heart attack in October 1959 it was revealed that Flynn had been in chronic health for some years. He had suffered from excruciating back pain (brought about by a fall several years earlier), malaria and also had to endure occasional bouts of tuberculosis and gonorrhoea. He had acute hepatitis and there was little left of his liver and kidneys. The coroner expressed amazement that Flynn had even managed to reach fifty.

It would be an exaggeration to suggest that there was an element of tragedy about Errol Flynn but there is no doubt that, on screen at least, he remained unfulfilled. It wasn't a case of the clown wanting to play Hamlet. It was simply that beneath the image of a hard-drinking, real-life swashbuckler lay a genuine actor trying to get out. For much of his career Flynn longed to be taken seriously but found that his public image – which admittedly he enjoyed fostering – and his screen persona kept hindering such ambitions. Whenever he suggested, usually tentatively, that he might perhaps be something more than just a guy with a sword or a machine gun in his hand he would be told by his studio to forget it and stick to what he did best. And what he did best was to romp with grace and style, and with amazing agility, through a series of swashbucklers that remain the best ever produced in Hollywood. Today, those entertainments are no longer acclaimed as they once were. Most of the time they seem naïve and shallow and lines such as 'Welcome to Sherwood my lady' bring about derisory amusement rather than an affectionate smile. Modern audiences, supposedly more sophisticated, reject them in favour of more violent celluloid adventures. Times change and films change with them. Nonetheless, even though his films belonged to a minor genre, Flynn did leave a rich legacy. No-one ever quite managed to take his place. He could wear period costume with devastating effect and he could combine panache with elegance and charm like no actor before or since.

Errol Flynn

Training for the swashbucklers! Errol Flynn preparing for his role in the 1936 Warner adventure The Charge of the Light Brigade.

He was born in Hobart, Tasmania, on 20 June 1909. He began in films after a career that was so colourful it would itself have made an excellent subject for a movie. According to his biography he worked his passage on several ships, prospected for gold, managed a tobacco plantation, hunted wild birds and smuggled diamonds. There was also a strong rumour, not substantiated, that he had once been charged with killing a man. When he later accompanied a sailing expedition to New Guinea his appearance in a movie of that trip led to an offer to play Fletcher Christian in a cheap Australian film of the Bounty mutiny, *In The Wake Of The Bounty*. Thereafter he was bitten by the acting bug and arrived in Hollywood after making a 'quota quickie' in Britain called *Murder At Monte Carlo*.

Considering the adventures of his early life it was not surprising that Flynn had acquired a taste for alcohol and the high life long before he signed for Warner Brothers. His dependency on alcohol was to prove a continuing problem throughout his career. Even when he had become a star as *Captain Blood* he still needed booze to boost his confidence and fortify him.

He was lucky to get the chance to appear in that film at all, for British actor Robert Donat had originally been cast and shooting had already begun when Donat had to pull out at the last moment. For Flynn it was a case of being in the right place at the right time. He'd made just two films for Warners, neither of them distinguished, and had been well down the cast list on both. When production chief Hal Wallis and studio boss Jack Warner decided that two other Warner possibles – Brian Aherne and George Brent – would not be right for the part they looked to Flynn. He wasn't a name but he had the looks, he was athletic and he was the right age. Besides they were desperate. The role Flynn was required to play was that of a physician who becomes a buccaneer in the reign of James II.

Hal Wallis remembered Flynn's screen test well. He said later:

He wasn't an admirable character but he was a magnificent male animal, and his sex appeal was obvious. It seemed not to matter whether he could act. He leapt from the screen into the projection room with the impact of a bullet.

His first day at work was astonishing. He arrived late, in a bad temper, with no idea of the lines he was to speak, and no idea of how to act them. He was to give a long speech in the hall of the Lord High Justice of England. But the results were better than we dared hope. Errol's delivery was extraordinary in its intensity and conviction. He was one of those rare personalities with whom the camera fell in love. He couldn't move or make a gesture that wasn't instantly photogenic.

About halfway through the picture he demanded that we rewrite his contract. He knew the excitement his performance was creating and wanted to take advantage of it. We were so impressed by what we had seen of him on the screen that we re-wrote his contract mid-picture and raised his salary to $750 per week. This became a pattern. Every time we started a picture with Errol he demanded an increase in salary. We had the choice of renegotiating the contract or not having him in the film.

Flynn wasn't overly impressed by starting his career with what he considered to be a run-of-the-mill pirate picture. When shooting finished for the day he was one of the first off the lot, usually heading for some bar or party or late night binge. Someone who witnessed the results of Flynn's off-screen exploits at first hand was the Warner make-up man Perc Westmore. Like the stars he had to be at the Warner studio early, making sure that they were in the right condition to work. Flynn gave him more problems than any other actor on the Burbank lot.

Westmore's brother Bud, who later worked as a make-up man for the Universal studio, recalled how Flynn would drive Perc to distraction with his cunning and ingenuity.

> Errol moved in fast company after studio hours. There was hardly a night when he didn't go drinking and was on the prowl for nubile females. In the morning he would report for make-up, bleary eyed and hung over, to be confronted by Perc, immaculately white-smocked, make-up tools in hand and glaring at him with clear-eyed virtue. On one occasion when my brother was particularly pensive and quiet over Flynn's delicate condition the actor shouted at him in desperation: 'Don't you ever do anything wrong?', to which Perc replied, 'No'.

Once Westmore had designed Flynn's make-up he would turn the actor over to one of his assistants and proceed with his next job on one of the other Warner stars. When one assistant took over, Flynn quickly subverted him and persuaded him to make certain substitutions in his make-up case. Gin replaced skin cleanser, hair preparations became bourbon and so on. Things worked out well for a while until Perc accidentally sniffed a Scotch-flavoured shaving lotion one day and summarily fired the duplicitous assistant. Flynn accepted defeat but only temporarily. He came to enjoy the cut and thrust with Westmore as much as did making the movie, probably more if truth be known. The challenge of finding new ways of getting a few 'belts' under his belt before venturing onto the set proved to be irresistible.

Flynn's next ruse was to order 'malted milks' at 6.30 every morning. The malts were, in reality, Ramos gin fizzes, consisting of nine parts gin and one part beaten egg white. When his make-up (and his malts) were finished he would swagger from his dressing room and onto the stage to swashbuckle as Captain Blood. Most mornings he tended to buckle more than he swashed. Westmore caught him again and banned 'malted milks' from his make-up room.

Flynn was only in his mid-20s when all this was going on. His erratic behaviour proved to be a constant source of worry to Jack Warner but if Warner entertained any hopes that Flynn would turn over a new leaf he was mistaken. The actor never reformed throughout his entire period at the studio.

There was one occasion when it seemed as though he had mended his ways when he began eating oranges every day, but it wasn't long before it was discovered that once again he had been conning everybody. He had been arriving on the lot ten minutes before everyone else and syringing the oranges with vodka.

Flynn finished *Captain Blood* in a relatively sober state which, all things

'You've come to
Nottingham once too often!'
'When this is over, my
friend, there'll be no need for
me to come again!'
*Flynn versus Rathbone! The
climactic duel from the classic
1938 swashbuckler* The
Adventures of Robin
Hood.

considered, was a good thing for after his success in the film Warners quickly cast him in one film after another, most of them swashbucklers. The genre had been virtually dormant since the silent heyday of Douglas Fairbanks and no-one had bothered too much with it in the 1930s, least of all the Warner studio which was more concerned with producing realistic gangster films and the kaleidoscopic musicals of Busby Berkeley. But once *Captain Blood* was released Jack Warner immediately broadened his schedule to include costume romance and 'cloak and sword' spectaculars. What followed were some of the most elegant swashbucklers of all time, the best among them being the rousing *The Adventures Of Robin Hood* and the superbly orchestrated *The Sea Hawk*. Flynn, hangovers and all, romped

▶ Errol Flynn with Bette Davis in The Private Lives of Elizabeth and Essex *(Warner Bros, 1939). The superb costumes were designed by Warner costume designer, Orry Kelly.*

his way through each and every one, seemingly born to play the swordsman and adventurer, his lithe athletic frame swinging from trees in Sherwood Forest and leaping across the staircases of Nottingham castle.

Flynn never considered his swashbucklers to be of any importance. It didn't impress him that he fenced with a grace that seemed almost poetic at times and that no-one else in Hollywood could match. He dismissed his achievements with an airy wave of the hand, preferring to enjoy himself in Hollywood deep into the night.

For a time he shared a rented house in Beverly Hills with his friend David Niven. They had begun in Hollywood at about the same time and boozed, womanized and smoked marijuana (then referred to as 'kif') together. The booze and the drugs and the women were hardly the right ingredients to keep Flynn in the best of shape but for a while at least his lifestyle didn't affect his screen athleticism. Occasionally during the morning rushes a discerning viewer would notice that Flynn didn't quite seem to be focusing as he should but if Jack Warner noticed he never commented. During the late 1930s Flynn got away with just about everything, both inside and outside the Warner studios.

His friendship with Niven came to a temporary close with the outbreak of World War II. Niven immediately volunteered and returned to Britain. Flynn did not. He felt no loyalty to England and very little to Australia. And as he'd already become an American citizen he felt under no obligation to go. When the Japanese bombed Pearl Harbour in 1941 he hesitated but again decided not to join up. Instead, he played mock war heroics for Warners who temporarily abandoned swashbucklers for war adventures, films which required less physical exertion on Flynn's part. One, *Objective Burma*, a fine film directed by Raoul Walsh, got him into deep trouble because it inferred that he had won the Burma Campaign almost single handed and without the help of a single British soldier. None of which was his fault, more that of the screenwriters who had put the story together, but it was he who was singled out for blame by the British press. The outcry was so great that the film was withdrawn from London's West End after just a few days.

Walsh, who directed the great majority of Flynn's films in the 1940s, became one of the actor's closest friends in Hollywood. He was a rough, tough, no-nonsense action director who went way back to the silent days when he himself had worked as an actor. He and Flynn had much in common. Their tastes were the same and so was their sense of humour. Flynn also felt comfortable with Walsh. On two occasions, when he played General Custer in *They Died With Their Boots On*, and the prizefighter Jim Corbett in *Gentleman Jim*, he showed that when he really tried (and according to Walsh he put a lot into both performances) he could rise above the normal one-dimensional portrayal he had been giving since reaching stardom with *Captain Blood*. 'He was a much better actor than most people realized', said Walsh. 'He really worked on those two pictures – really worked. And he got good notices. If the studio had given him more of the same, perhaps things might have turned out differently.'

In The Adventures of Robin Hood *it was Basil Rathbone who played the villain, here it was Henry Daniell, but the result was the same: death for the latter!* The Sea Hawk *(Warner Bros, 1940).*

Warners however, still looked on Flynn, first and foremost, as a swashbuckler and after the war put the clock back ten years by casting him in *Adventures Of Don Juan*. It soon became painfully obvious that he was no longer the man he had been in the days of *The Sea Hawk* and *The Adventures Of Robin Hood*. Vincent Sherman, the film's director, recalled that Flynn could only shoot twenty seconds of a duelling scene before he had to cut. By then Flynn was gasping for breath. Flynn had enjoyed boasting that he had done all his own stunts on *Robin Hood* but it was Fred Cavens who did much of the swordplay on *Don Juan*.

Sherman also remembered that Flynn's drinking had reached horrendous proportions on *Don Juan*. He said:

> He would show up at nine, go to his trailer and then not appear again until eleven. By then he had been fixed up with a shot by some doctor and was ready for work. But by the late afternoon he was usually smashed again.
>
> Character actor Alan Hale was another who liked to indulge quite heavily. One afternoon when we were shooting on location close to the studio we were beginning to lose the light. We needed some scenes of them on horseback. I decided to save time and return to the studio and use wooden horses and shoot against a backdrop. By the time we were ready they had come back from a very late lunch and both were well gone. I had the assistant director holding Hale onto his horse and the property man holding onto Flynn. They were so drunk that if either man had let go they would have fallen off. They laughed so much I had to shoot one line at a time. Somehow it worked. When you saw the finished picture you didn't know but it was a lot of trouble.

Flynn's drinking grew progressively worse as the 1940s wore on. So too did his womanizing. He was never without female company. The younger they were the better. Yet, many who were close to him felt that he distrusted women. Vincent Sherman believes that he didn't even like them very much and that he even feared them. David Niven thought that he treated them like toys, to be discarded whenever a new model came along. Raoul Walsh remembered that there was scarcely a woman in Hollywood who was not attracted to him. Walsh also enjoyed recalling the only occasion, in his memory, that a woman actually walked out on the actor. It happened when Jack Warner sent Flynn and Walsh to New York to drum up some publicity for *Objective Burma*. Warner had asked Walsh to act as chaperon and to try and keep Flynn under control. Walsh knew that this was well nigh impossible but agreed to do what he could. The minute they arrived Flynn began to behave in the most extravagant manner, forgetting that they were there to work for the studio and treating the trip as a kind of Roman holiday. He immediately placed an order with room service for ten bottles of Johnnie Walker, eight bottles of Gordon's, half a dozen bottles of vodka and champagne, two of them on ice right away. Next on the list was caviar, Guinness stout and three dozen oysters. As he put the phone down he added 'if there are any pretty girls in the lobby send *them* up too'

◀ *Flynn at his swashbuckling peak as the adventurous Captain Geoffrey Thorpe in the film that many regard as the finest in the genre,* The Sea Hawk, *directed by Michael Curtiz.*

Raoul Walsh remembered quite vividly what happened next. He said:

Errol called a friend of his, a very famous stockbroker in New York. The stockbroker told him he was giving a party that night at his house and wanted Errol to come. So we went to the party and Errol spotted a beautiful society girl and he went right after her. The romance lasted for about five or six days.

Everything was charged to his room so he ordered six dozen roses to be sent to her in the morning and six dozen in the afternoon all the time we were there. Then he ordered bonbons and chocolates to be sent. And he eventually ended up sending her two French poodles that cost $500 apiece.

After about five days I came back from visiting some friends and he was down in the dumps. He was drinking brandy straight out of the bottle and was so drunk he could hardly talk. When I asked him what the matter was he said 'She walked out on me'. Well this was the first girl that had ever walked out on *him*. He generally did the walking. It shocked him. So I said, 'Forget it, what the heck?' He focused on me in a wobbly way and said: 'She won't talk to me on the phone or see me so I'm going to jump out of the bloody window.'

I took the bottle away from him and mentioned that it was a little late to commit suicide. He agreed to wait until the morrow. 'I'll do it though. You better believe me.' He passed out then, after I had promised to go and see the girl. He was snoring gently in his chair when I went down to the bar to get away from him.

When I got back to the suite, he was wide awake. 'Did you see her?', he asked, 'What did she say?' I said: 'She wanted to know what time you were going to jump so she could come and watch.'

That was the end of the brief romance. What Flynn called the girl was unprintable. The hotel bill came to more than $6000 and a good deal of it was for American beauty roses. We flew back to Hollywood because Flynn said trains were for peasants.

Walsh also came to Flynn's assistance when Jack Warner threatened to break the actor's contract because of his bad time keeping. According to Walsh the studio boss actually phoned down to the police at the gate so that he could check on the time Flynn arrived in the morning. Walsh said:

I heard about this. My house wasn't very far from his house up on Mulholland Drive, so I went up and told him and I said, 'Look, you're in trouble and I know you need the money. You bought this $100,000 yacht and you've got a crew on it. I'm going to pick you up at seven thirty every morning and take you through the gates so that you can register in, then you can go to your dressing room and I'll have some coffee sent to you. Take a nap for about an hour and I'll work with somebody until you are on your feet.' He put his arms around me and kissed me and said, 'You're my only friend'. Then I'd go up there at seven o'clock in the morning to pick him up, and I knew he always had some girl or somebody there. I didn't want to go in and embarrass anybody. He had a Russian butler, so I'd say, 'Alex, is anybody in there?' and he'd reply, 'Oh, no, Miss So-and-so just leave.' And some of the names he told me would astound you.

If Walsh saved Flynn from making a fool of himself in minor ways it was lawyer Jerry Giesler who came to his aid on a much more serious matter some three years earlier. Late in 1942 Flynn was arrested on four charges of Statutory Rape. Two girls, supposedly eighteen but looking all of twenty-two charged that they had been deflowered aboard his yacht *The Sirocco*. In California statutory rape meant that a male had fornicated with a female below the age of eighteen. Naturally enough the headlines read 'Robin Hood charged with rape' and naturally enough the two girls, Peggy Satterlee and Betty Hansen made the most of their brief time in the limelight.

Both girls were well upholstered and mature looking which did little for the validity of their case. The prosecution ordered them to remove their make-up, do their hair in pig tails and carry school books. Giesler quickly tore away the pretence raking up their tacky past (and there was plenty to rake up) and showing what a mockery the trial was. Peggy Satterlee's account of her supposed seduction or rape aboard *The Sirocco* brought the house down when she said that Flynn had whispered in her ear that 'the moon would look more beautiful through a porthole'.

When Betty Hansen took the stand and testified that Flynn had taken off her clothes Giesler asked her pointedly: 'Didn't you want him to take them off?' Betty's disarming reply was: 'I didn't have no objections.' Errol Flynn was acquitted on all four counts by the jury, nine of whom were women.

The trial, unlike that of Charlie Chaplin some two years later (in which Giesler again played a prominent part) became something of a joking point. 'In Like Flynn' was an expression used frequently in everyday conversation, especially by army personnel, and the whole business came as a welcome *divertissement* to the war news.

The Warner studio however in no way considered the trial to be a laughing matter. Flynn was a valuable asset and still one of their top money-making stars. Flynn also breathed a sigh of relief. If he'd been found guilty it would have meant a prison sentence of five years and that would almost certainly have meant the end of his career. He later revealed that had he been found guilty he would have hopped aboard a plane and left the country. After the trial was over the general consensus was that the whole affair had been a put up job and that Flynn had been made a scapegoat by the Los Angeles District Attorney who wanted to discipline the film community for its lack of morals. The two girls, it was assumed, had been bribed to make their testimonies.

The trial cost Flynn $50,000 in hard cash. He became the butt of jokes of scandal journalists and night club comedians. 'In Like Flynn' was to stick with him for the rest of his career. For the most part he took it all in good humour and went along with the jokes. At least on the face of it he did. Close friends said that the jokes hurt him more than he cared to admit.

In 1946, in an attempt to break away from his mundane film roles, he turned to writing. Most unusually he seemed to enjoy the solitary occupation. He had started writing newspaper articles in New Guinea, and, when he became well known as an actor, wrote for a number of magazines. His first book *Beam Ends* was an amusing account of his voyage up the east coast of Australia in 1930. He also co-authored a screenplay called 'The White Rajah', sold it to Warners and was disappointed when they didn't use it.

His most ambitious work, apart from his autobiography *My Wicked, Wicked Ways* (published posthumously) was a novel called *Showdown*. It was partly autobiographical and concerned the adventures of a young Irishman in the South Seas. The critics were lukewarm, claiming it to be overwritten. When a *New York Herald Tribune* reporter asked him why he had spent so much time writing a book when he obviously didn't need the fame or the money, Flynn replied: 'I got more of a kick out of writing it than I do out of making pictures. That's the only explanation I can give. It helped me get rid of a sense of futility.'

There was nothing in Flynn's final years to indicate that things would change for the better. There were more swashbucklers at other studios (each worse than the one before), a couple of musical disasters in England when he teamed with Anna Neagle in *Lilacs In The Spring* and *King's Rhapsody*, and an abortive attempt to enter film production with *William Tell*. Even here luck deserted him. He invested $430,000 of his own money, half of the film's estimated budget, and cast himself as the legendary Swiss hero. Intent on making the picture a quality production he brought in Jack Cardiff to photograph and direct and even decided to use the then brand new CinemaScope process. Shooting had been in progress for only a few days when Flynn learned that his Italian partners had reneged on the agreement and pulled out, leaving Flynn to find twice as much again. With the United States Government also claiming some $840,000 in back taxes he found himself close to desperation. Shooting continued as Flynn tried to find new backing but after six weeks filming in Northern Italy production ceased. Flynn tried to interest Harry Cohn of Columbia, Herbert Wilcox and others but he could get no further. Some 30 minutes of footage was shot. None of it has ever been shown publicly.

It is too fanciful to suppose that had *William Tell* succeeded it would have given Flynn a new start, maybe behind the cameras as a producer or executive producer. Many stars were launching into independent production in the 1950s and most of them found the new found freedom to their liking. Whether Flynn would have had the patience though is doubtful. And in any case, by 1954, even though he was only 45, he was too far gone in health. He was a habitual drug user and had begun to experiment with heroin. He was a total alcoholic and a physical wreck. He remained bitter about his film career and seemed to yearn for his younger days before he arrived in Hollywood. In a magazine article he wrote:

When I first came to Hollywood, I enjoyed whatever fame I had, but gradually it began to pall on me. The days of my poverty and vagabondage come back to me now with a nostalgia that has the force of a blow. It's pleasant to remember I had few worries then and practically no responsibility. I felt rich when I had accumulated twenty five dollars. No-one had invested millions in me, and the jobs of others were not dependent on me. It was pleasant to be carefree and irresponsible...I frequently find myself restless and rebelling inwardly at the deadly

▼ *Errol Flynn (centre) as matinée idol John Barrymore in* Too Much Too Soon *(1958).*

routine of picture making. I get the feeling that life is slipping by me – that time is passing and I am not living fully.

Ironically, just prior to his death in 1959, he made something of a comeback, appearing in three successive films as an alcoholic. 'Typecasting again', he muttered to one journalist when asked about his roles. 'They say it's the new Flynn but it's not. I'm still playing myself just as I always have.' All of which was true up to a point but as the boozy, happy-go-lucky bankrupt Mike Campbell in *The Sun Also Rises*, actor John Barrymore in *Too Much Too Soon* and the guilt ridden British officer who has betrayed some fellow officers to the Nazis in *The Roots Of Heaven*, Flynn was more than effective. There were indications even that he might have developed into a formidable character actor.

Errol Flynn

◄ *A unique hiding place for the booze! Flynn discovers some much needed refreshment in* Too Much Too Soon, *the story of the life of Diana Barrymore. Flynn starred as John Barrymore who, like Flynn, drank himself to death.*

The last of these three films, *The Roots of Heaven,* was directed by John Huston and was adapted from the prize-winning book by Romain Gary. The novel was a fine piece of work, the film was a mess, almost certainly because most of it was shot in French Equatorial Africa where temperatures were 140 degrees by day and 90 degrees at night. Most of the cast and crew fell ill with malaria, amoebic dysentery and other tropical diseases. Only Huston and Flynn came through the ordeal relatively unscathed. Huston had been a buddy of Flynn's since the 1930s when he'd worked first as a writer and then as a director at the Warner studio. In those days the pair had often drank and scrapped together. When filming *The Roots Of Heaven* Huston sensed the end was near for the actor even though he'd lost none of his old ingenuity in fixing himself up with what he needed for the location work. Huston said:

> Errol Flynn was truly ill but it had nothing to do with Africa. He had a vastly enlarged liver. He continued to drink, however, and was on drugs. He knew he was in bad shape, but he put on a great show of good spirits. He'd brought along some fine French wines, potted grouse and various delicacies from Paris – and plenty of vodka. I remember seeing Errol sitting alone night after night in the middle of the compound with a book, reading by the light of a Coleman lantern. There was always a bottle of vodka on the camp table beside him. When I went to sleep he was there, and when I'd wake up in the middle of the night I'd see him still sitting there – the book open, but Errol not reading any longer, just looking into his future, I think, of which there wasn't very much left.
>
> The company doctor came round to see me one day and told us he wasn't going to give Errol any more drugs. He said that he felt professionally obligated to take this stand. We concurred, so Errol found himself another doctor – a French army doctor who'd been at Dien Bien Phu. We discovered in short order that he was unfettered on such things as ethics.
>
> I used to hear cats meowing at night, and I wondered why I never saw any cats. Then I discovered that the French doctor was supplying Errol not only with drugs but with girls as well. The girls came round at night and signalled their presence to Errol by meowing. He would open his door furtively and let them slip in. All these young ladies had been given bismuth treatments for venereal disease by the French doctor and pronounced eligible for Errol's delectation.

All of this occurred just a year before Flynn's death in 1959. He did make one other film, a fourth-rate little semi-documentary called *Cuban Rebel Girls* in which he played himself and which co-starred his 17-year-old girlfriend of the time, Beverly Aadland. It was as much a mess as he was himself and not a film he would have chosen as his epitaph.

When he died on October 14, 1959 the world was not shocked or surprised and, as usual, the tributes flowed in from all those who had known him or worked with him on his pictures. Olivia de Havilland recalled: 'He was a charming and magnetic man, but so tormented, I don't know about what, but tormented.' Greer Garson said: 'He was more objective and modest than most performers. He was satirically deprecating about himself. If he had lived longer – and more temperately – he would probably have emerged as the serious actor he longed to be'. Ann Sheridan: 'He was one of the wild characters of the world but

▶ *Errol Flynn with Beverly Aadland, his last girlfriend, at her seventeenth birthday party in September 1959. Flynn died just a month later.*

he also had a strange, quiet side. He camouflaged himself completely. In all the years I knew him, I never knew what really lay underneath and I doubt if many people did.' Jack L. Warner, his old boss (and rival) at Warners, said: 'He had a mediocre talent but to the Walter Mittys of this world he was all the heroes in one magnificent sexy, animal package ... Actor or no actor, he showered an audience with sparks when he laughed, when he fought, or when he loved. He was one of the most charming and tragic men I have known.'

Earl Conrad, the man who worked with Flynn on his frank and entertaining autobiography *My Wicked, Wicked Ways* perhaps summed him up best when he wrote:

> He had too much fortune, too much adulation, too much sensual indulgence, too much everything. Finally he was consumed by it all. Then he had the problem of living up to the reputation he had come by as an international fun figure, as a colourful personality who should provide headlines for the public every few weeks or months. This produced in him a great tension and strain. It all helped to give him an image he didn't really want and in time he became a ripped-out-at-the-seams, caricature of himself.

▼ *Close to the end! Errol Flynn, not at his best, with 17-year-old Beverly Aadland.*

Whether Errol Flynn could have become the actor he seemed to want to be or whether his yearnings in that direction were all a bit of a sham is difficult to know. Certainly in his later films he did indicate that he had a modicum of talent but by then he was filled with both remorse and self pity. He chose to roister and enjoy his personal life and let the professional side of things slide until it was too late to stop. He seemed to discover this halfway through his career and the net result was that he lived the last years of his life regretting what might have been. Raoul Walsh certainly thought of him as a fine actor when he directed him at Warners in the 1940s, not too many others did.

He was arguably the most self-destructive actor who ever worked in Hollywood. He rode his luck in the early years of his career but when the genre that had brought him fame became suddenly *passé* he found that life in front of the cameras became more difficult. He never achieved any ambition on screen yet he is still remembered as the most heroic of swashbucklers and one of the most elegant of men. When he suffered a mild heart attack during the making of *Gentleman Jim* his co-star of the film, Alexis Smith, remembered a remark that indicated his fatalistic attitude toward life. 'Everyone was more concerned about it than he was,' she said. 'I told him, "You'll have to take care of yourself. Don't you want to live to be an old man?" He said, "No, I like this half of life best and I want to live it to the hilt." '

4. Judy Garland

Judy Garland

Judy Garland in her early years at MGM.

Judy Garland was a show business phenomenon; a brilliant singer with an instinctive talent, she was a child star who graduated through adolescence into womanhood without once taking a break from the screen. By the time she was 28, an age when most movie stars were reaching their peak, she was regarded as a has-been, a burnt-out case.

When MGM at last let her go in June 1950 no-one was unduly surprised. She'd been at the studio for nearly 15 years and had appeared in almost 30 films, most of them musicals. She had sung 'Over The Rainbow' in *The Wizard Of Oz*; co-starred with Mickey Rooney in *Babes in Arms*; danced with Kelly and Astaire; and appeared for Vincente Minnelli in the movie that began MGM's Golden Age of musicals, *Meet Me In St. Louis*. By the mid-1940s she was unquestionably the finest musical talent the cinema had produced. Yet even then she was heading for destruction. In 1950, shortly after being suspended by her studio, she made the headlines by slashing her throat with the jagged edge of a broken bottle.

The reasons for Judy Garland's decline have been discussed and analysed by many biographers yet none has been able to come up with a satisfactory conclusion. Some argue that Judy's mother, Ethel Gumm, an ex-vaudevillian and the personification of the pushy, ruthless show-biz mum, was the primary cause. Certainly Judy herself held no love for her. She said:

> Mother was the real-life wicked witch of the west. Mother was no good for anything except to create chaos and fear. She didn't like me because of my talent. She had a crude voice and my sisters had lousy voices too. When I review my financial problems, I have to admit they began with my mother.

Others have maintained that Judy's insecurity stemmed from the fact that she failed to find true happiness with any of her five husbands, including Vincente Minnelli, and that, despite the marriages, she was forever lonely. Most though, blame things on her studio. She was just fifteen when she first signed for MGM. Studio boss Louis B. Mayer didn't like her at first, referring to her as his 'little hunchback'. But once he saw what she was capable of he was merciless. He put her on the studio treadmill and never once allowed her to step off. Lyricist E.Y. Harburg said:

> In Hollywood Judy was a commodity. She was there for exploitation. When they saw they had a moneymaker, they used her to the hilt – unwisely and inhumanely, with no conception of the psychological treatment of a human being. This was common in the industry. If the star was box-office one year, that didn't mean he or she would be box-office the next. So the studio wanted every ounce of profit they could get.

The pressure on Judy Garland was more intense than that inflicted on other MGM stars because most of her films were musicals. In the beginning these musicals required only the occasional song or two. Then they demanded dancing. After that a lot of singing and a lot of dancing. No other film genre required so much rehearsal or drained so much nervous energy. Judy coped at first. The excitement kept her adrenalin going and brought her musical performance to a

▶ *Judy Garland and Mickey Rooney; MGM child stars who appeared in ten films together during the late 1930s and early 1940s.*

fine edge. But even in those early years the studio made sure she didn't miss a day in front of the cameras. Judy later recalled:

> They'd give us pep pills. Then they'd take us to the studio hospital and knock us cold with sleeping pills. After four hours they'd wake us up and give us the pep pills again. That's the way we worked and that's the way we got thin. That's the way we got mixed up. That's the way we lost contact.

Exactly when Judy Garland first became addicted to pills is another of the imponderables. Legend has it that she was using them as early as 1939 when she was just 17 and filming *The Wizard Of Oz*. But those who worked with her remember that it was in the early 1940s that things first became noticeable. Gene Kelly, who appeared with her in *For Me And My Gal*, said:

> She had a great capacity for laughter. She laughed and she wanted to laugh. There were no complications to her. If she had the beginning of a problem at that time, I don't think anyone knew it. I suppose hindsight would tell me that there were signs even then. But no-one was looking for them.

One of the first people to notice that things were beginning to go badly wrong with Judy Garland was Joseph L. Mankiewicz. In 1942 he was a writer and producer at MGM. Although married, he became romantically involved with Garland who was then making the difficult transition from child to adult star and was newly separated from her musician husband David Rose. Mankiewicz said later:

Mickey Rooney presenting Judy Garland with a special Academy Award for The Wizard of Oz *for 'the best juvenile performance of the year'.*

She was enchanting. In many ways I'd never met anyone like Judy at that time. I'm not talking about her talent. She was just the most remarkably bright, gay, happy, helpless and engaging girl I'd ever met.

By and large, the women I knew or had relationships with, were as neurotic as I was. It was not unknown to find neurotic women and men in show business. One thing a neurotic male or female dearly loves is to have his or her neurosis discussed, preferably by another neurotic. I knew that Judy's behaviour patterns revealed that she was in trouble. She was full of unconscious hostility toward the parent, represented by the studio, which she manifested by not showing up on time. They told her she was a hunchback. Christ almighty, the girl reacted to the slightest bit of kindness as if it were a drug. We think of Judy as a really big star but she was pushed around, she was treated by most people, including her mother, as a *thing*, not as a human being.

One of Mankiewicz's close friends at the time was the psychiatrist Dr Karl Menninger. Mankiewicz drew his attention to Garland's problems and asked him to talk with her. Menninger told him that she did need urgent help and, because she was only 20, there was no reason to suppose that she couldn't handle things – always providing that her problems were brought into the open and she was made to recognize them. Had she been allowed to do this its possible that Judy Garland might have been able to cope with life rather more easily than she subsequently did.

Unfortunately for Mankiewicz, his friendship with Garland came to the notice of Louis B. Mayer. When he was returning to the studio after visiting Menninger in Topeka, Mayer was on the same train. He immediately summoned Mankiewicz to see him. It was night-time. Mankiewicz said:

> I went to see Mayer in my slippers and bathrobe. A screaming fight ensued. First he accused me of wanting to have an affair with Judy and that I was just making believe I was her friend. Then he accused me of fucking around with Judy. He was absolutely uncontrollable in his rage and said something to the effect: 'I won't have it'. Then, at the end, in the typical L.B. Mayer fashion, he said: 'You have to understand. I have the welfare of all my players at heart, and I'm talking to you like a father.' I said, 'No, you're not. You're talking like a jealous old man,' and walked out of the compartment. That's what really generated L.B.'s hatred, I think

That was the end of round one. Round two began back at the studio when Mankiewicz, who felt that he didn't deserve to be berated in such a fashion, demanded an apology. He didn't get one. Instead, he found Mayer was at him again. This time he suggested that Mankiewicz was meddling with Garland's mental health. Psychiatric care was not what Judy needed, he said. The studio and Judy's mother knew perfectly well what was best for her. Mayer also told Mankiewicz that Mrs Gumm had complained to him about her daughter's visits to Menninger and that she believed he was twisting her daughter's mind and alienating her affections. Mankiewicz, unable to conceal his anger, stood up and said: 'Obviously Mr Mayer, this studio isn't big enough for both of us.' Seconds later he realized the full implications of what he had said. Mayer was the boss of the studio, Mankiewicz an employee. Mankiewicz left shortly thereafter. Judy stopped seeing her psychiatrist and her affair with Mankiewicz gradually petered out even though they never stopped being friends. Later, those close to her, said that she was so depressed over the break-up she began taking pills even more heavily than before. She never stopped singing one of her favourite songs 'Happiness Is Just A Thing Called Joe', she named her son (by a subsequent husband – Sid Luft) Joseph and in later years would often phone Mankiewicz late at night in moments of distress.

For his part, Mankiewicz believed the affair ended because of Judy's affection for another man working on the lot, director Vincente Minnelli. Minnelli had been at MGM for some three years and first directed Judy in the non-musical *The Clock*, a slight wartime romance co-starring Robert Walker. He was also selected to make her next film, the nostalgic, turn-of-the century family musical *Meet Me In St. Louis*. It was during the shooting of this film that Minnelli noticed Judy using some form of medication. He had no idea where she was getting the pills or who was supplying them, but he was not one of those who believed that it was the studio. Minnelli said:

> The unions, during Judy's early years at the studio,weren't as powerful as they later became. Everyone put in long hours. Some fellow actor, trying to be helpful, probably offered some amphetamines to Judy during one of those especially long days. It probably wasn't long before she herself was seeking them out to see her through many fourteen-hour work days. The pills left her wide awake, unable to sleep, so somebody else offered her a sedative. Few people knew about the long

▶ Meet Me In St Louis *(1944), the film that began the golden age of MGM musicals.*

range effects of such drugs at the time. By the time of *Meet Me In St. Louis* the working conditions were more humane and Judy shouldn't have needed them any longer. But she continued using them.

But even if MGM hadn't been responsible for putting Judy on drugs (and Minnelli's case is only supposition) they certainly had no idea of how to get her off them. It's doubtful if they even tried. They had more stars on the payroll than any other studio in Hollywood. The problems of one star, no matter how talented, were not their main concern. They simply worked her harder. And the harder she worked the more pills she took. For Judy, it was a 'Catch-22' situation. Minnelli was always able to tell if she'd taken Benzedrine the night before or that morning. Like other actresses using the drug she would come on set, deliver a song and believe that it was the best rendering she had ever given. Minnelli knew that it was not; there was always something about the performance that wasn't quite as sharp as it should have been, something that was slightly off centre.

When Minnelli and Garland married in 1945 there was a period, albeit a brief one, when Judy did make a conscientious effort to stay off medication. Minnelli realized there was no way he could force her to stop but he did try gentle persuasion. When they were in New York on honeymoon Judy took a vial of pills and hurled it into the Hudson. She asked him to hold her hand and told him softly that that was it. No more pills. For a while Minnelli believed her, especially

15 June 1945; the wedding of Judy Garland and Vincente Minnelli. Studio boss Louis B. Mayer (left) gives his blessing.

when their daughter Liza was born in March of the following year and for the first time Judy found herself occupied with things other than her career.

It was when she came back after the birth of Liza that things took a turn for the worse. Up until then Judy had always had a canny knack of knowing just how far she could go with the MGM executives. She knew just how many hours she could miss, just how many times she could be late and still keep the film on schedule and within budget. No film she had been in had suffered unduly because of her illnesses or tardiness. Then came *The Pirate*, an ambitious Technicolor version of the Broadway play by S.N. Behrman. The Lunts had appeared in the Broadway production; Gene Kelly and Judy were to star in the film version which had the additional bonus of a new score by Cole Porter. In every way it was a major production. Arthur Freed was producing, Minnelli directing.

Judy Garland and Gene Kelly in the Cole Porter number 'Be a Clown' from The Pirate *(1948).*

Shooting became a nightmare. Judy worried incessantly about the lavishness of the film, about playing a sophisticate rather than her usual girl–next–door role, and whether she was in the right 'mood' for such a musical. She became edgy at home, even more anxious on the set – when she deigned to turn up. For much of the time she didn't. Sometimes she would arrive for a couple of hours' rehearsal and then leave. On other occasions she would arrive in the morning and leave just an hour later. Sometimes she would not appear at all and the company was left wondering just what they would do when they had finished shooting around her.

Minnelli could sense that she was back on pills but made no reference to the subject either at home or at the studio. The worst moment during the shooting occurred when she arrived to shoot the expensive 'Voodoo' number which she had pre-recorded just two days earlier. When she saw that she had to act on a set full of open fires she became hysterical. 'I'm going to burn to death', she screamed. 'They want to burn me to death.' Minnelli, embarrassed, tried to reassure her but she tore herself away from him and ran to a group of extras, asking each one in turn: 'Do you have some Benzedrine?' Finally, she broke down in tears and had to be led sobbing from the set.

Many of those who were there that day had known Judy for years. They had heard of her problems but the subject never came up in conversation. It was always something to be avoided. But after the outburst on *The Pirate* Judy's fragile health had become plain for all to see. She was only 25 but even then it was not difficult to see that the end was coming.

The Pirate took seven months to shoot and it came in half a million dollars over budget, mainly because of Judy's problems, which even included a row with

'Tramps', Judy Garland and Fred Astaire, in the Irving Berlin number 'A Couple of Swells', Easter Parade (MGM, 1948).

Cole Porter, usually the most amicable and generous of men. The row ensued over a couple of songs she had to sing in the picture. The first was 'Love Of My Life'. When she arrived for the recording she was under drugs and unsteady on her feet. At times she seemed as though she was in a trance. Porter was present at the recording. She sang unnaturally slowly. Porter made a polite comment but was unusually evasive. When she recorded the second song 'You Could Do No Wrong' Judy could barely get through it. Porter insisted that she was not doing justice to the word 'caviar.' There was an argument about whether the emphasis should be on 'ca-vi-ar' or 'ca-viar'. Judy became unreasonable. Voices were raised and it needed all the calming influence of vocal arranger Roger Edens to calm things down.

Through all of this Minnelli had to think of his own career and about trying to save his marriage at home. Although near exhaustion point himself, he contented himself with the knowledge that the next Judy Garland vehicle, *Easter Parade* (again to co-star Gene Kelly) would be a much less ambitious affair, a simple, schmaltzy tale of a Broadway hoofer who is let down by one dancing partner and then finds another, a small-time singer/dancer in a chorus. It never occurred to Minnelli that he would not get to direct the film. He had assumed that he would be directing all of Judy's musical pictures at the studio from then on. That this was not to be the case became all too obvious when he was called to Arthur Freed's office, just a few weeks before rehearsals were due to begin. Freed looked embarrassed. Minnelli thought he had decided to scrap the picture. Instead, Freed said: 'Vincente, Judy's psychiatrist thinks it would be better all round if you didn't direct the picture. He feels Judy doesn't really want you as the director, that you symbolize all her troubles with the studio. You can't be both her director at work and her husband at home.' Minnelli, shocked and hurt, for Judy had said nothing to him, withdrew from the film. He never directed Judy again.

As things turned out it was Fred Astaire and not Gene Kelly (who broke an ankle a month before shooting) who co-starred with Judy Garland in *Easter Parade*. Perhaps that was why she managed to get through the film without any trouble; Astaire, an older man and brought out of retirement for the picture, might have been a calming influence. Or maybe it was because she felt more in charge of things without Minnelli on set. The new director, Charles Walters, was a former choreographer who had directed only one other film, *Good News*. When the two met for the first time Judy greeted Walters with: 'Look sweetie, I'm no June Allyson, you know. Don't get cute with me – none of that batting the eyelids bit or fluffing the hair routine for me, buddy. I'm Judy Garland, just you watch it!'

It was said in jocular fashion and Walters took it that way but it seemed that Judy wanted to assert her own authority and by doing so lessen her anxieties. Whatever the reason, the whole thing worked to perfection. The filming of *Easter Parade* passed off without incident and the picture became MGM's most successful post-war musical.

The same team – Garland, Astaire and Walters – were brought together for a

follow-up movie called *The Barkleys of Broadway*. Like *Easter Parade* it was a lightweight affair, a soufflé of a film that had more musical numbers than plot lines. Work began in June 1948 but during the second week of rehearsals Judy began to falter and by the third week she was back in the same nervous condition she had been in when filming *The Pirate*. The pills again took control, she became edgy and nervous and her weight would fluctuate alarmingly from one day to the next. Arthur Freed, knowing that he could not allow a repeat of *The Pirate* fiasco, contacted Judy's doctor. He sent a memo to Mayer about her condition. It read:

> Subject/Judy Garland – illness/July 12, 1948. 3.30 p.m. Memorandum of telephone conversation with Dr. Schelman to ask how Miss Garland was and he said he had given her medication to help her sleep. I asked him, in his opinion as her physician, if it would be wise to start her working in an important picture. He replied that it would be a risky procedure. He said that she possibly could work four or five days, always under medication, and possibly blow up for a period and then work again for a few days. He was of the opinion that if she didn't have to work for a while it might not be too difficult to make a complete cure but that her knowledge of having to report every morning would cause such a mental disturbance within her that the results would be in jeopardy.
>
> I told him that I was anxious for Judy to get well and he volunteered to come in and have a talk with me. He thanked me for my interest and courtesy in the matter.

Freed had no choice but to take Garland off the picture. His memo revealed the enormity of Judy's problems and also those of the studio. For them she was still a much valued star; musicals made money and she was an essential part of the Freed musical unit at MGM. But musicals were also expensive. They took longer to make than other pictures and they had to be brought in on schedule. A star in Judy's condition was simply too much of a risk. For her part, Garland had reached the stage where she needed to be nursed, cossetted, treated gently, not because she was temperamental but because that was the only way she could function.

She struggled through another Charles Walters vehicle *Summer Stock* but then found herself cast in one of the studio's biggest ever productions, the film of the Irving Berlin stage hit *Annie Get Your Gun*. The film proved too much for her. Not only was she required to sing more numbers than usual she also had to play a role other than Judy Garland. Up until then her parts had usually been variations of the homely and innocent Judy; in *Annie Get Your Gun* she was cast as a real life character, the raucous sharp-shooter Annie Oakley. Worse still, Busby Berkeley was brought in to direct. He and Garland had never got along since he first directed her in *Babes In Arms* in 1939 when she was still in her teens. Berkeley was a shouter. He liked to roar on set. The only direction he would give Judy was 'OK. Do it!' to be followed by, 'Your eyes, yes, your eyes. Open them wide. I want to see your eyes!'

After a few days of shooting Judy went into the projection room to watch the rushes. She glared at what unfolded before her and then sank deeper into her seat. Then, with an expression of total disgust, she went to the water cooler and threw

▶ *A three-year old Liza Minnelli with her mother during the filming of the 1950 musical* Summer Stock.

▼ *'Get Happy', for many Garland's finest number on screen, from* Summer Stock.

a handful of Benzedrine into her mouth. Like Arthur Freed she knew it was awful. Berkeley had no idea what he was doing. He was shooting the film as if it were a stage musical. And she was totally miscast. Freed fired Berkeley and brought in Walters. But by then Garland was more depressed than ever. Again there were absences from the set. In the end she was put on suspension. Betty Hutton was brought over from Paramount to replace her and the film was eventually directed by George Sidney.

Freed made one last attempt to save Judy's career by casting her with Fred Astaire in *Royal Wedding*. But by then everyone's patience had been exhausted and when, after just a few days, the same old pattern of lateness and absence began repeating itself, Freed and company decided that enough was enough. On 17 June 1950 Judy was put on suspension for the last time. Two days later she drew attention to her plight by locking herself in the bathroom of her home and cutting her throat with the jagged edge of a broken medicine bottle. But it was not a suicide attempt, just a gesture, a futile cry for help. She had drawn the glass only lightly across her skin, just enough to draw blood. Nothing worse.

In September, three months after her suspension she was let go (not as is sometimes believed sacked) by Metro-Goldwyn-Mayer. She had been 'owned' by MGM for all but two days of the preceding 15 years. She never made another picture for the studio.

Vincente Minnelli, in an attempt to explain Judy's open hostility towards MGM from *The Pirate* onwards said:

> Judy had come to feel that all she represented in the studio's mind was top grosses. The paternal feeling Metro executives held for her, she now felt, was all tied in with how much money she could bring in. Their genuine displays of affection for her were seen as a contrivance to get her to perform. Again she felt betrayed and nothing I could say could dissuade her from that notion. In the back of her mind, she was concocting schemes of revenge for such treachery. She proceeded to get even not by lashing out, though those who were the targets of her caustic tongue felt otherwise. The anger turned inward, seething uncontrollably, threatening to destroy Judy herself... the sweetest and most perverse revenge of them all.

Judy herself remembered the traumas of the early years:

> No wonder I was strange. Imagine whipping out of bed, dashing over to the doctor's office, lying down on a torn leather couch, telling my troubles to an old man who couldn't hear, who answered with an accent I couldn't understand, and then dashing to Metro to make movie love to Mickey Rooney.

Most thought that Judy Garland, with her erratic work habits, would never make another film after she left MGM. It would be too much of a risk for any studio to hire her and too much of a risk for her to prove to herself that she could still perform. But four years later, after a series of successful concerts at the Palace in New York and the Palladium in London, her third husband (a former test pilot named Sid Luft) put together a deal with Warner Brothers to film a remake of *A Star Is Born*. Garland played a young singer on the way up who is turned into a

▲ *Comeback! A Star is Born (Warner Bros, 1954): Judy Garland sings 'The Man That Got Away'.*

major film star by a middle-aged actor on the way down because of drink. James Mason co-starred as the actor Norman Maine. Jack Carson and Charles Bickford made up the cast.

Warners and Luft poured a great deal of money into the 'comeback' picture. George Cukor was brought in to direct and allowances were made for Judy's unreliability. Delays were allowed for and it was a wise move. Four years' absence had not improved things. Sometimes there would be no Judy. On other occasions there would be Judy for just an hour or two. There would also be times when she would turn up in the evening because she felt she could only function at night. But, even allowing for the inevitable, the budget costs still rose alarmingly. Sometimes, when Judy had not turned up at all, Cukor would make a great fuss over directing James Mason arriving in or leaving in his studio car, just to suggest to the Warner studio heads that they were actually filming something – even though they were in reality filming nothing at all.

James Mason said:

> The higher ups tended to forget that they had undertaken this operation knowing full well that Judy did not have a reputation for reliability; they forgot that prizes are not won nor audience bewitched by an exercise in reliability. Henry Hathaway used to say that to bring in a film under schedule was not going to make it a hit. Producers and directors strove to come in under schedule because they were afraid of the studio boss. To get something as unique as Judy's talent, some patience and certain sacrifices were needed. If the film went over budget, only a very small fraction of the overage was due to Judy's erratic timetable. When I think of it, my God they were well off! Judy was by no means a temperamental star. 'Temperamental star' is usually a euphemism for selfish and bad tempered, and a temperamental star of this sort can be a *real* time waster. I have worked with some. But this was not Judy.

As Mrs Norman Maine Judy Garland was, for the first time, required to prove that she was not only a fine musical performer but also an effective and emotional actress. Her dramatic scenes in the picture earned her an Oscar nomination for best actress of the year. She was lucky in having at her disposal a director of the quality of Cukor who had drawn some outstanding performances from actresses in the past.

Cukor said:

> Until *A Star Is Born* Judy Garland had only played in musical comedy. A lot of people in musical comedy are like mimics or impersonators, which is not real acting. They promise more than they deliver. You think: 'If only they could play out a scene, how good they'd be' and very often you're wrong.
>
> But Judy Garland was a very original and resourceful actress. Toward the end of shooting we had to do a scene when she's in a state of total depression after her husband's suicide. While we lined it up, she just sat there, very preoccupied. We'd talked about the scene only a little, but we both had a general idea of what it should be.
>
> The basic note was her melancholia, her state of total depression. Just before the take I said to her very quietly. 'You know what this is about. You really know this.' She gave me a look, and I knew she was thinking, 'He wants me to dig into myself because I know all about this in my own life.' That was all. We did a take. In the scene she has trouble in articulating anything, she seems exhausted and dead. A friend, played by Tommy Noonan, comes to see her to try and persuade her to go to a benefit performance that night. He chides her about not giving in to herself, he even gets deliberately rough with her – and she loses her head. She gets up and screams like someone out of control, maniacal and terrifying. And when Judy Garland did this, it was *absolutely* terrifying. She had no concern with what she looked like, she went much further than I'd expected, and I thought it was great.

Great or not, Cukor asked her to do it one more time, just for a slight change of emphasis. The second time was as convincing as the first take. 'You really scared

▲ *James Mason, Judy Garland and Charles Bickford face the Hollywood Press. A scene from* A Star is Born.

the hell out of me,' said Cukor. He later added:

> She was very pleased, she didn't realize what an effect she'd made. And she was always funny, she had this great humour. She said: 'Oh, that's nothing. Come over to my house any afternoon. I do it every afternoon.' Then she gave me a look and added: 'But I only do it *once* at home.'

If *A Star Is Born* had not been hacked down from its original rough cut of four hours to three-and-a-half then two-and-a-half it might well have emerged as a great picture. Even in its truncated form it remains the most satisfying film of Garland's career and arguably the best ever made about Hollywood. If Judy had won the Oscar instead of Grace Kelly (who was named for *The Country Girl*), if Sid Luft had produced more pictures for her, as he had intended . . . Unfortunately, as far as Judy Garland was concerned there were always too many

Judy Garland and James Mason on location for A Star is Born.

A dramatic Judy! As the tragic Irene Hoffman under cross examination by Maximilian Schell in Stanley Kramer's Judgment at Nuremberg *(1961).*

Judy Garland with a sympathetic Dirk Bogarde in I Could Go On Singing *(United Artists, 1962).*

'ifs'. Even if she had won an Academy Award there is no way of knowing whether it would have brought her luck and started her on a new career in pictures. She did make more films – there were two more straight roles in *Judgment At Nuremberg* and *A Child Is Waiting*, and another musical, *I Could Go On Singing*, her last, which she made in London with Dirk Bogarde.

But mostly it was Judy Garland the stage entertainer who captured the headlines during the last fifteen years of her life. That and her successive marriages to actor Mark Herron and nightclub manager Mickey Deans, both men younger than herself. Even for live performances she would be late, causing much anger to those in the audience who had paid a large admission price to see her perform. On one occasion she kept an audience waiting for an hour and twenty minutes

Judy Garland

before she went on. Sometimes she would confide to people that she would do it deliberately so that she could get the adrenalin going, walk onto the stage and then, through her talent, make them forget they were angry with her and eventually applaud her.

She died in London on 22 June 1969 from an accidental overdose of sleeping tablets. She was 47. When the news of her death flashed across the world the tributes, the summings-up, the explanations of her problems all came tumbling out once more. In the end it was almost certainly MGM that killed her. They didn't seek to ruin her deliberately. That would have been counter-productive. But they were in the business of making money and stars were really no more than well-dressed dolls to put on screen and help them make that money. Film-making in Hollywood in the 1930s and 1940s was a tough business. If you were hard and could take the knocks you could survive the studio machine and go on to the next picture. If you weren't strong, were blessed with a stroke of fragile genius and didn't know how to handle the 'business' side of film-making, then you were almost certain to go under. And that's what happened to Judy Garland. Vincente Minnelli said of her: 'She was an actress, plagued by the temperament and insecurity which affects every great one. She simply couldn't help being what she was.' A critic described her as being constantly 'at war with herself. She was very bright and sensitive and constantly aware of her shortcomings. The well of nervous energy on which she had to feed needed constant replenishing.'

Judy Garland drew on all her resources for 47 years. When she died she had been through it all. She had a God-given talent but had a fear of performing. She suffered from anxiety to a torturous degree and lived on the prolonged verge of a nervous breakdown. Most of all she had a neurotic fear of loneliness. What she suffered and what she brought on herself would have made a lesser person an invalid. It's a tragedy that she was not allowed to develop her prodigious talent on stage where it would have emerged at a slower pace and allowed her to mature as an artist. Making pictures, especially in the studio days, was always a hasty business. Judy Garland suffered from being pushed too far and too fast by a ruthless studio machine. The reward was stress, fear, anxiety and just a few moments of private happiness. Generally, her personal life seemed more like an out-of-control roller-coaster ride, a fruitless search for the happiness promised in 'Over The Rainbow', the song she made famous in *The Wizard Of Oz*.

When she died she was in debt to the tune of a million dollars despite having earned more than eight million during her career. When asked what it was he thought killed Judy, her *Wizard Of Oz* co-star Ray Bolger gave the simple answer: 'She didn't die of anything, except wearing out. She just plain wore out.' E.Y. Harburg put things rather more poetically when he summed up her life:

The American fantasy called 'success' eluded Judy. Making a film is gruelling excitement every minute. It's an unnatural environment. She had no life – no vacations – she was there to be applauded and toasted every minute. She had only tinsel, nothing real.

5. Sterling Hayden

Sterling Hayden

'The most beautiful man in the movies'. Twenty-four-year-old Sterling Hayden photographed at Paramount Studios in 1940.

If Sterling Hayden had been a wiser man he would have devoted his life to the sea rather than taking up acting as a career. The sea and sailing ships had been his first love since he was a boy of sixteen. But, as he liked to recall in his later years, he was not a wise man. Indeed, in his own eyes he was a very foolish one. After making his first round-the-world-voyage when he was twenty, and earning his first command just two years later, he allowed the lure of an easy life in Hollywood to entice him away from what he cherished most. The rewards were not great. He appeared in a series of trite films and then, when the chips were down and he was required to stand up and be counted, he was found wanting. He 'sold out' to the House Un-American Activities Committee. In 1951 he admitted to a brief membership of the Communist Party, betrayed many friendships and had to live with the consequences of his actions until his death some thirty-five years later.

All of which would have been tragic enough had Hayden been an ambitious actor hellbent on winning an Oscar and carving out a major niche for himself on screen. Selling out to advance his livelihood would at least have given him a motive, no matter how reprehensible his actions. But Hayden could not even use that as an excuse. For him, acting was simply a means to an end. He'd had no training and at one stage had considered staying in Hollywood only long enough to buy his first ship. Just why he felt the need to inform and safeguard a career for which he had nothing but distaste remained a mystery, not only to Hayden's friends but also to Hayden himself.

He first arrived in Hollywood in 1940 after a talent scout had spotted his photograph in the *Boston Herald*. Paramount soon billed him as 'The Most Beautiful Man In The Movies' and 'The Beautiful Blond Viking God' which indicates the kind of movies they had in mind for him. Depending on his mood Hayden would either laugh or shudder at his early efforts in front of the cameras. His own view of his acting performances, even those late in his career when he gave several notable portrayals (the mad base commander in Kubrick's *Dr. Strangelove*, the Italian patriarch in Bertolucci's *1900*) was that they lacked range. When quizzed about this he would simply shrug, refuse to elaborate and say in his typically colourful manner: 'Quite frankly I didn't know what the fuck I was doing'.

He probably didn't know too much about what he was doing when he volunteered for service in World War II but at least his war record was one of the few things in his life of which he was tolerably proud. He said: 'It had more twists and turns than the plots of my first two films, *Virginia* and *Bahama Passage*, put together – and then some.'

He trained first, semi-officially, with British commandos until he broke his leg in a parachute jump. After that he conducted Hemingwayesque small-boat operations in the Caribbean. Then came a spell in the Marines and with the Office of Strategic Services. He worked in Intelligence in several countries including Yugoslavia where he assisted Tito's partisan guerillas. He was cited for his bravery, winning the Silver Star, and was also honoured by Tito himself.

It was his involvement with the partisans that led him to embrace Communism when he returned to Hollywood in 1946. He said:

> I wanted to do something for a better world. If I could do something about the condition of the world, I could probably justify my position as an actor with a good salary and good working conditions. As I began to operate in Hollywood after the war I continued to talk, almost incessantly about this thing built up in me by the Partisans in Yugoslavia. We established a close personal feeling with these people. We had unlimited respect for the way they were fighting. Our plane crews would leave their shoes with the Partisans they were that impressed.

Unfortunately for Hayden those in high places in the States were no longer impressed by the Yugoslavs nor by any of the countries behind the so-called Iron Curtain. Countries that had been allies just a year before were suddenly enemies. The Nazis had been vanquished, the Communist scare was on. Anyone who was labelled 'red' or 'pink', or was even faintly liberal in their views, was accused of being subversive.

Hollywood was investigated first in the late 1940s when writers and directors (notably the 'Hollywood Ten') were indicted; then in the early 1950s when it was the turn of the actors to face the inquisitors. Hayden was one of the first. His day came on 10 April 1951. The usual newsreel cameras and microphones (over 30 of them) were on hand to record the event. Hayden later summed up what he had to say on that day as 'a crockful of shit' which is as succinct a way as any of describing his testimony some of which went thus:

> I would like to say I appreciate very much, very very much, the opportunity to appear here today. I think there is a service to be rendered, not only to the country at large but to those who find themselves in a similar position to mine. I have heard there are hundreds of thousands of ex-Communists who don't know what to do about it. The suggestion made by the chairman of this committee that people come up and speak is extremely fine, constructive. My appearance before this committee could serve a very useful purpose.

The words were not Hayden's, they were concocted by his lawyer but Hayden ploughed on with the testimony even though he did not believe a single word of what he was saying. In his much acclaimed autobiography *Wanderer* Hayden wrote,

> Not often does a man find himself eulogized for having behaved in a manner he himself despises. I subscribed to a press-cutting service. They sent me two thousand clips from papers, east and west, large and small and from dozens of magazines. Most had nothing but praise for my one shot stoolie show. Only a handful – led by *The New York Times* – denounced this abrogation of constitutional freedoms whereby the stoolie could gain status in a land of frightened people.

Just how many people were frightened by the McCarthy witch-hunts was indicated all too clearly by the number who did admit to left-wing leanings and named names. The only ones to show courage were those who told the Committee that they reserved the right to remain silent, claimed the Fifth

▲ *Ground controller Sterling Hayden (second from left) instructing Dana Andrews on how to land his charter plane when two pilots are stricken with food poisoning. A scene from the 1957 production* Zero Hour *based on an original story of Arthur Hailey. The film was later spoofed in* Airplane.

Amendment and refused to inform on their friends. Many who did so were blacklisted and never worked in Hollywood again. Others, notably writers, did find work but had to operate under pseudonyms and sell their work under the counter at cut price rates. Some returned to acting in off-Broadway shows. Others were unable to find work of any kind. There were also those who committed suicide.

Most of those who did inform were later anxious to overlook the courage of those who had stood their ground. Invariably they would find some reason, no matter how trivial, to excuse their actions and ease their consciences. Hayden, to his everlasting credit, was not one of them. Just days after his testimony he was letting off steam to the psychiatrist who was treating him at the time and threatening to take a double-page advertisement in the trade papers admitting that he was still a Communist and that so were a lot of others. When the psychiatrist asked him why he didn't go ahead, Hayden who was then about to get a divorce from his second wife, replied desperately: 'Because I haven't got the guts. Maybe because I'm parlour pink. Because I want to remain employable in this town to finish this fucking analysis. Because when it comes time for the divorce I'd like to be able to see my children and the courts downtown are full of judges who would look askance at a divorced man who was an ex-Communist to boot. That's why.'

Hayden's reward for telling all at the Un-American Activities hearings was to read headlines such as 'Hayden Confesses', 'Ex-Red Hayden Bares Commie Past' and 'Hayden Washes Out Red Taint!' Materially his reward was to be handed a series of B-Pictures by Paramount, films with such titles as *Flaming Feather, Hellgate* and *Denver And The Rio Grande*. Occasionally something worthwhile would come along such as Robert Wise's adaptation of Edna Ferber's *So Big* and the Hollywood story *The Star* with Bette Davis, but then it was back to more of the same – *Kansas Pacific, Arrow In The Dust, Battle Taxi*, etc.

◄ The heist that went wrong. Sterling Hayden with the fatally wounded Anthony Caruso. A scene from John Huston's 1950 classic The Asphalt Jungle.

▼ Treachery among thieves! Sterling Hayden, Brad Dexter, Louis Calhern and criminal mastermind Sam Jaffe in The Asphalt Jungle.

Even before the traumas of 1951 Hayden's career as an actor was by no means distinguished although there was one picture that had offered him the slight hope that he might, after all amount to something in Hollywood. It was an MGM production called *The Asphalt Jungle*, a gangster picture about a jewel heist that goes wrong. What made it different to the normal run–of–the–mill crime film was that it took a sardonic view of crime as a branch of capitalism. What made it special from Hayden's point of view was that it was being directed by John Huston, then one of the hottest directors in town.

Hayden was both surprised and scared when he learned that Huston wanted him for the role of Dix Handley, the muscle man for the jewel thieves. The part required him to make a screen test and he recalled with horror his first day on the

set of *Virginia* when there had been undisguised laughter at his amateurish behaviour in front of seasoned professionals. The chance of working with Huston, however, overcame his trepidation. There was also the chance that the film might give him a start and allow him to pick his own projects.

Huston revealed to Hayden that MGM hadn't really wanted him for the role of the doomed hoodlum but that Huston had insisted. MGM eventually agreed but only if Hayden did a good screen test. When he saw how nervous Hayden was Huston simply told him not to worry about a thing. 'I'm not going to tell you how to play it', he said. 'Just do it your way and be comfortable with it.' Whereupon he relaxed in his director's chair, opened a book and began to read. After a couple of minutes hesitation Hayden took the plunge and for the first time in his acting life found himself coming to terms with a script that was literate and had some penetrating things to say about life in the criminal underbelly of urban America.

The test was successful, Hayden was accepted by Metro and *The Asphalt Jungle* was acclaimed as one of Huston's finest films. Unhappily it did not make money. Had it proved to be a financial success then the ensuing years might have turned out differently for Hayden. The film was released in May 1950, roughly a year before Hayden's appearance in front of the Un-American Activities Committee. At that time the actor had no way of knowing whether or not the film would turn out to be a moneymaker and whether enticing offers might evolve once other studios had assessed his performance in the film. It's possible that, at the back of his mind, he entertained a vague hope that he might, after all, make a go of it as an actor and that if he didn't testify and name names that chance would have gone for good.

But that is only conjecture. What is fact is that Hayden's career in the 1950s did not blossom. He made over thirty pictures all told, only one of them, a neat little thriller called *The Killing*, being of any quality. It was directed by the then up-and-coming Stanley Kubrick. The story of a racetrack robbery it again featured Hayden as a doomed criminal, a lower-class loser who almost but not quite manages to break free from his mundane way of life. Hayden learned a lot from Kubrick. He said:

> My agent was on the set one day, and he said, 'This is some bright kid from New York, and he's supposed to be good but he's full of shit.' But Stanley, he didn't care. He didn't pay any attention to anyone. He just did exactly what he wanted to do. The only trouble was he didn't give very much to the actors. On *The Killing* he was like a computer. A very talented artistic computer. Very detached. Obviously he knew exactly what he was doing, but he was preoccupied with the technical aspects of things.

In 1959, on a sudden whim and with his second marriage on the rocks, Hayden decided to do a Paul Gauguin and head in his sailboat for Tahiti. None of which would have caused much of a fuss if he'd have done it on his own. It made the front pages however when he decided to take his four pre-teenage kids with him and didn't return for almost a year. Although he had been given custody of the

▼ *Sterling Hayden in violent mood in Stanley Kubrick's 1956 thriller* The Killing.

children his wife had taken out a court action to prevent him from taking them on the trip. Eventually Hayden returned broke and disillusioned. He said later:

> I kept trying to break away. That's why I went to Tahiti and stayed. Then I came back. That was my mistake. I thought, my God it has to be fascinating for the kids. Well, maybe it sounded attractive, sailing to Tahiti, but it was also like a 102 ft prison for them with father at the wheel and no way to get away.

▶ *Sterling Hayden (as General Ripper) and Peter Sellers (as Group Captain Lionel Mandrake) in* Dr Strangelove *(Stanley Kubrick, 1964).*

In his later years Hayden never concerned himself about money. The only reason he would return periodically to Hollywood was to pick up the odd dollar to pay a bill. 'I'm enamoured of the idea of living marginally', he said.

> Security is a dangerous thing. I have no money. I've made a lot but never invested it or owned anything. Except ships. I've had 18 of them. I never owned a house. Bill Holden and all the other actors I started out with finished up as millionaires. Most of the time I have no more than a hundred bucks to my name.

He became a wanderer in the 1960s and 1970s not bothering too much with films and appearing in only those roles that appealed to him. One offer he had no hesitation in accepting was Stanley Kubrick's invitation to return to movies after a five-year absence, in the black comedy *Dr Strangelove*. His role was that of a deranged base commander who has a brainstorm and sends B-22s on a raid to drop atomic bombs on Russia.

Sterling Hayden

Once he had accepted the part however, his old fears about his acting abilities once again began to trouble him. Kubrick was mellower and warmer than he had been on *The Killing* which, as far as Hayden was concerned, was a good thing. The film was a nerve wracking experience. Hayden never forgot the days he spent on the film. He said:

I only worked for a week or two. I began to blow. I'd seen actors blow. H.B. Warner who played Christ in Cecil B. De Mille's *King of Kings*, was the worst. It was embarrassing to watch him. And I'd been to 8,12,14 takes. But this goddam thing with Kubrick was different. The more you retake, the more insecure you feel. We went 48 takes and I was dying. I was sitting there. I had the big cigar. I was sweating and I wished to do rather well. Well, we went to 48 takes. In the end Stanley said, 'We'll do pickups, sentence by sentence by sentence.' I couldn't even do a sentence. I was pouring with sweat. I went up to Kubrick and said, 'Stanley I apologize to you.' He said, 'There is nothing I can do to help you. But, and this is only a possibility, it might just be that the terror in your eyes might be useable in the film. If it doesn't work then in two or three months time you can come back and we'll do it again.' Well it must have worked because I never went back. People said to me: 'You were brilliant in that scene you're acting was superb'. Acting my ass. It was terror.

▲ *Off set on* Dr Strangelove. *Peter Sellers, Sterling Hayden and Stanley Kubrick.*

Dr Strangelove ushered in a new career for Hayden as a character actor. He was then 48 and no longer resembled Paramount's description of him as 'The Most Beautiful Man In The Movies'. Instead, he was rugged, stockier and rather more menacing. He declined to live in Hollywood, preferring to wander as the mood took him. One of his favourite cities was Paris where he would live on the Dutch barge he had moored on the Seine. His opinion of Hollywood never changed. Back in the 1940s, when he first began in movies, he described it as a place where they produced films that had formula stories that had no values or ethics. In the 1970s he couldn't wait to get away from the place. 'Everything is wrong with that city', he said. 'It epitomizes everything that's wrong with life.'

His feelings of guilt over his role in the Un-American Activities period never left him. He often willed journalists to bring up the subject if they were afraid to raise it in an interview, just so that he could exorcise a little more of his guilt. He never managed to clear his conscience but he never stopped trying. John Huston said of him in his memoirs: 'Sterling made a mistake and paid for it. His courage later made him a much finer human being.'

Shortly before he died Hayden summed it up thus:

I'm not ashamed of my career as an actor even though I've starred in a lot of terrible films. I did most of them for the bread. But I am ashamed of my betrayal. It still hurts me. I feel as guilty as hell even though I knew the Communists were using me. I was told that I was the biggest name they had. They realised that if I could be manipulated properly I could do some good.

Hayden would boast that if making a movie meant interfering with his way of life then that movie would get the thumbs down. He refused the Robert Shaw role in *Jaws* as he had done when he was offered Shaw's role of the gambler in *The Sting*. 'You'll have to shave off your beard', they told him. 'Fuck you Jack',

▼ Death of a Patriarch! Sterling Hayden as the peasant overseer Leo Dalco in Bernardo Bertolucci's Italian epic, 1900.

was his response and that was that. He also turned down three weeks in Bermuda and 195,000 dollars to appear in *The Deep*.

One picture he was sorry he *did* make was *The Godfather*. He hadn't grown his long beard by then and the part only required him to be in New York for five days. He had but a handful of scenes before being shot through the forehead by Al Pacino and finishing up headfirst in the soup. He said, 'I'm astonished at the number of people who seemed to enjoy *The Godfather*. I never saw it, never wanted to see it. I don't like violence. I was very unhappy on that film. I'm a scared human being; terrified all the time. It was absurd of me being up there playing a tough New York Cop.' Not quite so absurd perhaps when you take

▶ *Alcoholic novelist Sterling Hayden reunited with wife Nina Van Pallandt in Robert Altman's* The Long Goodbye *(1973), an updating of the Philip Marlow private-eye novel by Raymond Chandler.*

into account Hayden's bravery in World War II and his part in helping the Yugoslavs in their fight against the Nazis. What really scared him of course was his lack of moral fibre when it came to another kind of courage; to stand up and be counted when his country was caught up in the worst hysteria it had ever known. Only after that was he really afraid.

In his final years Hayden was a genuine eccentric, a tall, gaunt, bearded figure who on occasion went so far as to carry a staff round with him. He never watched his old films and carried a blanket with him to cover the television set in hotel rooms. He showed the effects of a lifelong relationship with alcohol and a ten-year affair with marijuana but he retained a keen interest in the world and events outside film-making. As a man he was warm, friendly, outgoing. He loved to talk of ships and the sea and his boyhood when he first sailed the oceans of the world. He would talk fondly of the women he had known (especially actress Madeleine Carroll whom he married after starring with her in his first two films) and, when pressed, even some of the films he had made. His favourite was Robert Altman's version of *The Long Goodbye*. 'It was a Raymond Chandler thriller. I don't remember a thing about making it as I was smashed at the time, but it's a good film and I'd like it as my epitaph.'

When he died of cancer in California in 1986 he seemed to have achieved rather more than he could have possibly hoped for when he was taking his first tentative steps in the film business back in the 1940s. His frank and courageous autobiography *Wanderer* and his novel *Voyage* proved that he was a fine writer and he had become an accomplished actor, at least in character parts. His range was limited but his performances for Kubrick, Altman and Bertolucci were solid and powerful. He was a troubled, contradictory man, a messed-up person who was always searching, drifting, hoping. He cursed the fact that he never had the courage to return to the sea. That's what he should have done but once Hollywood had got hold of him he found it difficult to break free. He said: 'I should have got on a Greyhound bus and gone back to Boston. Instead, I stayed in Hollywood and complained. That made me neurotic. Hollywood screwed me up.'

Back in the 1950s when Hayden made most of his films the cinema-going public knew nothing of the actor's troubles nor anything of his political battles of the time. Nor could they have cared less if they had. For them Hayden was just another Hollywood hunk, a two-dimensional hero of junk movies. But that wasn't an entirely accurate picture of Sterling Hayden. He wasn't perhaps an idol in the sense that Gable or Tracy or Peck were idols but he did make over 40 films in as many years and he left a handful of good performances that still bear viewing today. In the end Hollywood and he remained uneasy bedfellows. Hayden lost and Hollywood won. Hayden fell from grace in his own eyes; after April 1951 he never again enjoyed the luxury of self respect. 'I was strong enough to rebel, not strong enough to revolt', he said with extreme bitterness. 'I spent a lifetime selling out. I always hated acting but I kept on acting. I was a commuter on a tinsel train.'

6. Bela Lugosi

Bela Lugosi

There aren't too many actors who have been closely identified with one role on screen. Sean Connery and Roger Moore are two who spring immediately to mind for their portrayals of 007. Johnny Weismuller for his Tarzan, Basil Rathbone for his Sherlock Holmes and Peter Sellers for Inspector Clouseau are others. All of these actors enjoyed and benefited from their long associations with their respective creations.

For the Hungarian-born actor Bela Lugosi, however, it was a different story. In 1931 he became the first genuine screen Dracula, played him just the once on film and lived to regret that he had ever done so. He became so dominated by his portrayal of Bram Stoker's Transylvanian count that he was quite unable to rid himself of its image. The role, which he had also played on the New York stage in the late 1920s, haunted him for the rest of his life. Late in his career he said: 'Where once I had been the master of my professional destinies, with a repertoire embracing all kinds and types of men, from Romeo to the classics of Ibsen and Rostand, I became Dracula's puppet. The shadowy figure of Dracula, more than any casting office, dictated the kind of parts I played.' He added bitterly: 'Never has a role so influenced and dominated an actor's personal life and private fortunes.'

When he died, on 16 August 1956, he was a broken man with few financial resources, a victim of drug and alcoholic excess. His fame had long since evaporated and his last film, *Plan 9 From Outer Space* was one of the most embarrassing failures ever made in Hollywood. And yet, for all this, people still remembered him. Even such Dracula successors as Christopher Lee, Frank Langella and Klaus Kinski, more frightening though they subsequently were, couldn't shake off the malevolent image of Lugosi. With his often absurdly exaggerated gestures, slow, hesitant speech, and his chilling reminder to the luckless visitors to his castle that 'I never drink – wine', he *was* Dracula.

For the Universal studio *Dracula* was a tentative re-entry into the horror market they had embraced so successfully in the silent days. Like most studios in the early 1930s they needed something to help them through the early setbacks of the Depression and horror films seemed the ideal solution to their problems.

They saw Lugosi as the natural successor to Lon Chaney and the ideal star to help launch their horror cycle even though they weren't exactly over-generous to the actor during the filming of *Dracula*. Lugosi was paid just $500 a week for seven weeks for his labours. He also received little or no thanks for his part in persuading the heirs of the Bram Stoker estate to accept $40,000 rather than the excessive $200,000 they had first demanded for the film rights to the novel.

Nonetheless, once 'The Story Of The Strangest Passion The World Has Ever Known' (as *Dracula* was advertised to the public) became a box-office hit, Universal went out of their way to make up for their niggardly treatment of their star. H.G. Wells' *The Invisible Man*, Robert Louis Stevenson's *The Suicide Club* and even Hugo's *The Hunchback Of Notre Dame* were all mooted as future Lugosi projects. So too was Mary Shelley's masterpiece *Frankenstein* which had then been filmed only once before, in 1910.

Bela Lugosi

Unlike Dracula, the part of Frankenstein's monster – a creature made from the organs of dead bodies – required considerable make-up. At first, none of this seemed to worry Lugosi. He entered wholeheartedly into the spirit of things, subjecting himself to rigorous tests by Universal's make-up man Jack Pierce. The public, fascinated by the personality of the strange new Hungarian star and anxious to know more about his next film, scoured the fan magazines for every detail. One trade announcement of the time informed them that:

Bela Lugosi, in the starring role, will be built up with make-up and padding, to resemble the eight foot superman Mary Shelley wrote about in 1818. When Lugosi is made up only his chin and eyes will be visible, greasepaint and putty completely hiding the rest of his face. Shoes to which nearly 12 inches have been added, complete the illusion.

The production was given an additional touch of class when Universal announced that Leslie Howard would play the scientist who assembles the monster and brings him to life.

It was after just a week of make-up tests that things began to go wrong. There are conflicting accounts of what occurred. One is that the test reels showing Lugosi resembling 'the golem' with his head about four times normal size were not well received by Carl Laemmle Jr, son of Universal's founder. Jack Pierce's explanation was that Lugosi was removed from the role because he had too many ideas that didn't coincide with those of the producer. 'Lugosi thought his ideas were better than everybody's', he said. For his part, Lugosi claimed that it was he who decided against the role. He felt that his public, who had taken to him in such a big way in *Dracula*, would be disappointed if they did not see his face on the screen. He said later: 'I turned down the role because of a lack of dialogue . . . I convinced the studio that the part did not have meat enough.'

The truth of the matter almost certainly lay somewhere in between but there's little doubt that Lugosi's high regard for himself had quite a lot to do with the eventual outcome and that his removal – or resignation – from the part had far-reaching effects. The role went to Boris Karloff, then an unknown bit player who had been languishing in Hollywood for years and had more or less given up any thoughts of ever achieving stardom.

Lugosi, still firmly convinced that he had made the right decision, agreed instead to play in another horror vehicle, *Murders In The Rue Morgue*, a bizarre film about a maniacal doctor who performs diabolical experiments with kidnapped women and a huge gorilla in order to prove his mad theories of evolution. Compared with *Frankenstein* it was a distinctly second-string production and it wasn't long before Lugosi realised the enormity of his mistake. In November 1931 *Frankenstein* was premiered to even greater acclaim than *Dracula*. Once the film went on general release Karloff was established as the number one horror star at Universal with Lugosi relegated to number two. The positions were never reversed. Lugosi's reign at the top lasted roughly eight months, from the St Valentine's Day release of *Dracula* to the November release of *Frankenstein*.

Lugosi's egotism was a not uncommon complaint among Hollywood stars of the time (or indeed since) and it was perhaps understandable. He sincerely believed that his popularity was due to his acting abilities whereas it was due almost entirely to the public's fascination with the vampire count he had played so successfully. The public seemed totally unable to distinguish between the actor and the character he portrayed on film. Lugosi also thought himself a much better actor than he really was. On the European and American stage he had played a wide variety of roles (including Shakespeare and Ibsen) and believed that even greater film success would follow after *Dracula*. He was disappointed and genuinely bewildered when it did not.

Viewed today, Lugosi's screen acting seems hesitant, stagey, unconvincing. Lines are spoken slowly, dragging out scenes that are meant to have pace. Had he

▲ *Somewhat less menacing! Lugosi's Dracula cowers before his destroyer, the Dutch scientist Professor Van Helsing played by Edward Van Sloan in* Dracula.

concentrated on trying to command the English language he might have succeeded but he never bothered. In Boris Karloff's view it was his biggest mistake as he recalled many years later.

> Poor old Bela. It was a strange thing. He really was a shy, sensitive and talented man. But he made a fatal mistake. He never took the trouble to learn our language properly. Consequently he was very suspicious on the set, suspicious of tricks, fearful of what he regarded as scene-stealing. Later, when he realized I didn't go in for such nonsense we became friends. He had real problems with his speech and difficulty interpreting lines. I remember he once asked a director what a line of dialogue meant. He spent a great deal of time with the Hungarian colony in Los Angeles and this isolated him.

Karloff and Lugosi were thrown together on seven occasions in the 1930s and 1940s. Most of their films were cheaply made flicks featuring mad doctors and scientists and sinister butlers. The subjects ranged from invisible rays and devil

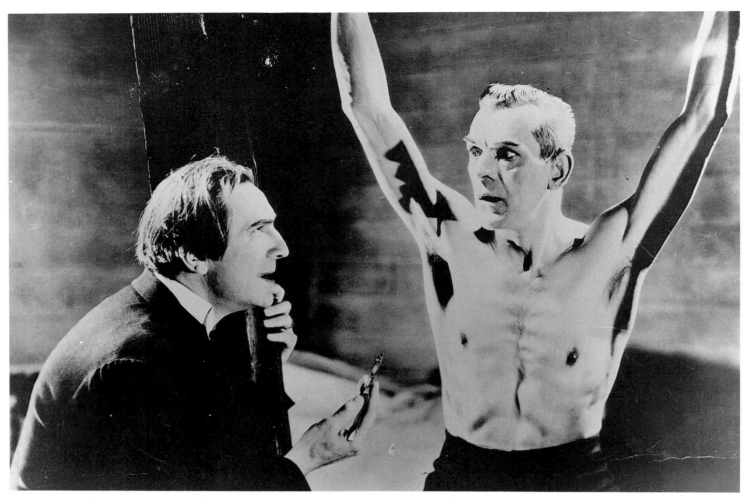

Son of Frankenstein *(Universal, 1939). Boris Karloff as the monster (his third and last portrayal); Lugosi as Ygor, the crazed shepherd who survives a hanging and becomes the monster's protector.*

Universal horror, vintage 1934. A vengeful Lugosi about to skin Boris Karloff alive in The Black Cat, *loosely derived from a story by Edgar Allan Poe and directed by Edgar G. Ulmer.*

A more convivial moment. Lugosi and Karloff relax between takes on the set of The Black Cat.

worship to grave-robbing. In one particularly sadistic film, Edgar Ulmer's *The Black Cat*, Lugosi was required to skin Karloff alive.

Ironically their most successful collaboration occurred in 1939 when they appeared in *Son Of Frankenstein*. Karloff appeared for the third time as the monster and Lugosi as Ygor, a crazy deformed shepherd who escapes the hangman and serves as the Monster's protector. Lugosi seemed to enjoy his role, possibly because he realized his character was bizarre enough to steal the film from Karloff. According to the film's director Rowland V. Lee, that is exactly what he did:

> Bela was greatly underestimated by the studio. We gave him his 'sides' as Ygor and let him work on the characterization; the interpretation he gave us was imaginative and totally unexpected. It wasn't Dracula at all, in fact, quite the opposite. He played Ygor as a rogue, but one who evoked sympathy. There was warmth in his voice and a twinkle in his eyes that made him almost lovable. When we finished shooting, there was no doubt in anyone's mind that he stole the show. Karloff's monster was weak by comparison.

Bela Lugosi

Lugosi made some 39 films during the 1930s. Only on one occasion did he step out of character when he played one of the three Russian commissars who enjoy the delights of Paris with Greta Garbo in Lubitch's comedy *Ninotchka*. He was adequate in the part but hardly gave evidence that he was an actor to be reckoned with when not starring in horror movies. Try as he might, he could not rid himself of the thought that Dracula, the role he had seized on so eagerly at the beginning of the decade, would never cease to be a burden to him. He said:

> Since *Dracula* Hollywood has scribbled a little card of classification for me and it looks as though I'll never be able to prove my mettle in any other kind of role. Not only have I a pathological leaning towards *Pollyana* roles, my one real ambition in life is to retire from the screen and settle down in peace and solitude on a little farm away from Dracula and other of my monsters.

It was an ambition that Lugosi was never able to realize mainly because he never had enough money to do so. He was either worth thousands or he was totally broke. There was never a halfway house. He enjoyed all the trappings that went with living in Hollywood and during the 1930s indulged himself to the full, living in luxury with his fourth wife in a handsomely furnished mansion. He earned a great deal, even though he appeared only in horror movies: but he spent even more. He entertained lavishly, ran a large car and wore elegant clothes. Studios encouraged their stars to live in such a style. When things went wrong as they invariably did and performers found themselves in over their heads the studios enjoyed even more control over them.

It was towards the end of the 1930s that things started to go badly wrong for Lugosi. The horror films that had been his regular source of income began to dry up as the public became bored with the same old stories and the same old sets. Lugosi was forced to grab at anything, simply to pay the bills. On one occasion he was even reduced to playing a mad munitions inventor in a 12-episode serial for Republic called *S.O.S. Coastguard*.

An additional burden was thrust upon him when his wife gave birth to a son. By then he was in serious financial difficulties: 'I had a fine big house, with plenty of servants and big automobiles. Then comes the non-horror fad. Bela cannot get a job. I lost everything. I lost my house and my cars and we move to a little house that I lease. Next comes the baby. I had not enough money to pay for it. Actor's Relief helped me pay for the baby.'

Things scarcely improved in the 1940s. If anything his movies, cut-price 60-minute efforts made for Monogram and producer Sam Katzman at Columbia, grew worse. Today, only movie buffs remember their titles – *The Corpse Vanishes, Night Monster, Ghosts On The Loose, Zombies on Broadway*. Only too well aware that his screen career was plummeting to the depths Lugosi endeavoured to earn extra money by returning to the stage. He appeared in a touring version of *Arsenic And Old Lace*, starred again as Dracula in a revival of the play which he took down the East Coast and even scored a moderate success when he featured in cross-country vaudeville tours.

▲ The Body Snatcher *(RKO, 1945). Karloff and Lugosi together for the last time in the Robert Wise version of Robert Louis Stevenson's gothic tale of grave robbing in nineteenth-century Edinburgh.*

With a career that was falling apart at the seams and a lack of adequate finance it was little wonder that Lugosi's health began to give way under the strain. He began to suffer from sciatica and in particular from extreme pains in the leg. His doctor prescribed pills to deaden the pain, but when he found that Lugosi was becoming too reliant on the pills he suggested that he come off the medication and opt for an operation instead. The operation was a success but Lugosi found himself unable to break the habit. Things became especially tough after he and his wife (of 20 years) were divorced in 1953. Two years later, in April 1955, he voluntarily committed himself to the Los Angeles County General Hospital for treatment to help fight his drug addiction. It was a courageous thing to do. Making public that you were addicted to narcotics was something that was more or less unheard of in the 1950s.

Bela Lugosi

When questioned about his motives Lugosi replied that he was broke and dependent on his friends for food and a small old age pension. He added that he was anxious to rehabilitate himself and had decided that committing himself to hospital was the only way to do so. During a Court Hearing the judge commended him for his honesty and committed him to the Metropolitan State Hospital in Norwalk for treatment.

It was while he was in hospital that Lugosi became involved with the woman who was to become his fifth wife.

Her name was Hope Lininger and her passion for Lugosi was decidedly stranger than many of the stories of his films. Back in the early 1930s, when Lugosi was at his peak, she had decided that one day she would marry Count Dracula. No doubt many women dreamed up similar fantasies about other screen characters only to forget them a week or two later. Hope Lininger was different. She held on to her fantasy and followed it through to its conclusion. Every move she made was designed to bring her closer to her hero. First she moved to Chicago, then on to Hollywood where she got a job as a cutting-room clerk at RKO. Finally, when she heard that Lugosi was ailing in hospital she wrote to him telling him not to give up hope. She wrote to him every day. When, in 1955, Lugosi was released, he not unnaturally wanted to meet the woman. They met, then married. The marriage lasted for just under a year until his death. She was 39, he was in his seventies.

After Lugosi's death Hope Lininger was interviewed many times about the last year in the life of Bela Lugosi. She told journalists all she could and could easily have made money out of her reminiscences. But she chose not to. After a while she grew tired of it all and wanted to forget that she had ever been Mrs Bela Lugosi.

When Lugosi died of a heart attack he was either 71 or 74 or 78, depending on which reference book you read. It seems more than likely that 78 was the correct age but there was no way of proving it one way or another. Over a hundred people attended his funeral. He was buried, according to his wishes wrapped in his Dracula cape. A young fan, knowing Lugosi's liking for cigars, stuffed one into one of his pockets. There were no famous names at the funeral.

In the end, Lugosi was a broken, decrepit old man, an alcoholic as well as a drug addict who hardly seemed to know where he was or what he should do with the rest of his life. Compared to Karloff who was fit and well and still proudly working in his late seventies, enjoying his cricket and his gardening, Lugosi was a shadow of his former self. His last film *Plan 9 From Outer Space*, was put together on a shoestring budget and filmed in and around a cemetery and in front of a house. There were no sets. The plot had something to do with resurrecting the Earth dead with a newly developed ray. Lugosi appeared briefly as one of those raised up. He appears in just a few scenes, for the film had only been shooting four days when he died. Another actor stood in for Lugosi in the scenes that remained to be filmed.

All told Lugosi made some 64 films. Of those only a handful are

Bela Lugosi, pictured four years before his death, in the British made Old Mother Riley meets the Vampire *(1952). The film co-starred comedy star Arthur Lucan and was eventually released in the USA in 1963 under the title* My Son the Vampire.

remembered – *Dracula*, of course, *Island Of Lost Souls* (a version of H.G. Wells' *The Island Of Dr Moreau* which he made with Charles Laughton at Paramount in 1933), *Son of Frankenstein*, and the final fiasco, *Plan 9 From Outer Space*. Not much when you come to sum it all up. Far less than most actors. Yet, today, more than thirty years after his death, *Dracula* remains the film that keeps Lugosi in the history books. Many find it difficult to accept that he played the vampire count but once and will sometimes argue the point quite heatedly. But although he appeared as other screen vampires Lugosi did indeed play Dracula on just one occasion in 1931.

It was then that a still optimistic Lugosi believed that success was just around the corner and that he was set for super-stardom. Thousands of letters were delivered daily to his home in California. According to Universal's publicity department 97 per cent of them were from women. The rest were from scientists and priests asking Lugosi's views on spiritualism, yoga and theosophy.

Commenting on the letters he received from women, Lugosi said:

> Women are interested in terror for the sake of terror. For generations they have been the subjected sex. This seems to have bred a masochistic interest – an enjoyment of, or at least a keen interest in, suffering experienced vicariously through the screen.

He also added:

> Other people would ask if my parents were hypnotists; if I communed with ghosts and whether or not I practised the supernatural in my private life. They said my eyes had an expression unlike the eyes of any human. As a matter of fact, my childhood in the Black Mountains was the usual, husky, healthy everyday life of any country boy. My father Baron Lugosi was a banker. There was nothing weird or extraordinary in my family background.

Nonetheless, even in his years of eclipse, people still liked to think there was and Lugosi would still receive the occasional fan letter inquiring about his background and if he was descended from vampires. It all seems a little quaint these days that an actor should receive so much adulation for just the one role. Vampires, and much worse, flit across our screens in a torrent of blood and gore that makes Lugosi's *Dracula* seem as though it belongs to another century. Little if any of the film stands up to more than a cursory viewing. Yet there was something, and there still *is* something, about that central performance that just occasionally chills the blood. The Satanic face, suave manner, the slicked down black hair and the malevolent personality serve to remind us that Lugosi has his place in film history even if Lugosi himself would have preferred that place to have been for a succession of parts that would have allowed him to demonstrate that he was indeed the actor he believed himself to be.

7. Marilyn Monroe

Marilyn Monroe

*◄ Marilyn Monroe,
Hollywood, late 1950s.*

Any taxi driver in Hollywood will tell you about Marilyn Monroe and that she once travelled in his cab. 'Right there, in that seat you're sitting in now,' he'll say, and then go into a long account of how he picked her up one night from a party and that, yes, she was every bit as glamorous as they said she was. All of it nonsense of course but as long as he can keep you hooked the cabby will keep at it, knowing the story will invariably result in an extra large tip. And the more bizarre the story the better, especially if it is embellished with sordid details of her tragic youth – her illegitimacy, her life in orphanages and foster homes and with a promiscuous mother who eventually went insane, her rape at the age of 8 by an elderly actor who gave her a nickel not to tell, her marriage at 16, her divorce at 20.

But the Monroe story, traumatic and harrowing though it is, is not really a complicated one. It's a tale of a girl who succeeded in becoming what she had always wanted to be – a world famous movie star – and then found that she didn't know what to do with her success. The stardom she hoped would bring her escape and happiness did nothing of the kind. It simply brought her more unhappiness, only this time her misery was caught in a relentless spotlight. Once she'd become established as another of Hollywood's sexy blondes she was trapped. Nurtured, promoted, expanded and generally confined within the stereotype, she found there was no escape from the image, except one, and she took that macabre route in August 1962 when she committed suicide in her Hollywood home.

Perhaps the most surprising statistic about Marilyn Monroe is that on only three occasions in the 1950s did she make it into the list of the top ten moneymaking stars. And never once was she the top moneymaking star in the world. In 1953 she was placed sixth after three films in one year had rocketed her to stardom; in 1954 she moved up a place to number five; and in 1956 she was ranked eighth after appearing in *The Seven Year Itch*. After that she never again figured in the moneymaking charts.

And yet her appeal to the public was enormous; her films were estimated to have made more than $200 million for her studio, and her innocent sexual vulnerability made her different from any other screen star before or since. Laurence Olivier said of her: 'She has a cunning way of suggesting innocence and naughtiness at the same time.' Joshua Logan remembered her as being 'the most completely realized and authentic film actress since Garbo. Monroe is pure cinema.' The director Jean Negulesco said: 'When she dressed to impress she was a hurricane of glamour. With a soft-spoken voice, helpless as a sharp knife, her eyes at half mast like a cobra watching its prey, she was a cruel child tearing off butterfly wings: gay, mean, proud and insatiable.'

Billy Wilder, who directed her in two major films and liked to boast that he'd lived to tell the tale, commented that she had 'flesh impact'. When asked to explain further, he said: 'Flesh impact is rare. Three I remember who had it were Clara Bow, Jean Harlow and Rita Hayworth. Such girls have flesh which photographs like flesh. You feel you can reach it and touch it.'

Yet not everyone found her attractive. Some who worked with her found her

▲ *Marilyn Monroe, starlet, 1950.*

◄ *Marilyn Monroe (just a year away from stardom) with Cary Grant in Howard Hawk's zany comedy* Monkey Business *(20th Century Fox, 1952).*

bitchy and selfish. Others thought she was ruthless, manipulative and inconsiderate to her fellow actors. Tony Curtis, who starred opposite her in *Some Like It Hot*, described his love scenes with her as 'like kissing Hitler'.

George Cukor, who directed her in *Let's Make Love* and was working with her on her last unfinished film, *Something's Gotta Give* when she was fired, said:

> There's been an awful lot of crap written about Marilyn Monroe, and there may be an exact psychiatric term for what was wrong with her – but truth to tell, I think she was quite mad. The mother was mad, and poor Marilyn was mad. I know people say, 'Hollywood broke her heart' and all that, but I don't believe it. She was very observant and tough-minded and appealing, but she had this bad judgment about things. She adored and trusted the wrong people. She was very courageous, she had to challenge the gods at every turn, and eventually she lost.
>
> When we made *Let's Make Love* I had no real communication with her at all. You couldn't get at her. She was very concerned about a lot of pretentious things – she'd done a lot of shit-ass studying – and I'd say, 'But Marilyn, you're so accomplished, you do things that are frightfully difficult to do.' She had this absolute, unerring touch with comedy. In real life she didn't seem funny, but she had this touch. She acted as if she didn't quite understand why it was funny, which is what made it so funny.
>
> In certain ways she was very shrewd. I once heard her talk in her ordinary voice, which was quite unattractive. So she invented this appealing baby voice. Also, you very seldom saw her with her mouth closed, because when it was closed she had a very determined chin, almost a different face. The face wasn't all that pretty, but it moved in a wonderful way, it was a wonderful movie face

Writer/director Nunnally Johnson who wrote the screenplay for *How To Marry A Millionaire* recalled:

> My conviction is that she just bored the hell out of everybody. She just didn't have the intelligence, and she was aware she didn't have it. That's why she'd buy Dr. Eliot's Five Foot Shelf of Books and why she was busy reading this writer and that. When she married Arthur Miller, my guess is that she wasn't smart enough for him.
>
> I found Marilyn difficult to talk to. I just couldn't get to her, or feel that I had established any kind of communication with her at all. Sometimes I didn't know whether she understood what I said. When I tried to talk to her, I felt as if I was trying to talk to somebody under water.

If Marilyn's studio, 20th Century Fox, had known how to make the most of her talents it's possible that things might have turned out less tragically for the blonde superstar. Yet, despite the shrewd business acumen of studio boss Darryl F. Zanuck, they hesitated about giving her the big break. From 1948 to 1952 she appeared in a dozen movies for the studio, most of them second string comedies in which she played minor roles. But only in *All About Eve* (in which she played George Sanders' protégée) and *The Asphalt Jungle* (for which she was loaned to MGM and featured as Louis Calhern's mistress) did she make any kind of impact.

In many ways being a Fox star proved to be something of a drawback. Had

▼ Robert Ryan with a 25-year-old Marilyn Monroe in the Fritz Lang drama, Clash By Night *(RKO), a film she made on loan out from Fox in 1952.*

she been at Warners or Paramount or MGM she might have stood a better chance but at Fox she was living in the shadow of Betty Grable, Zanuck's blonde pin-up girl of the 1940s. Zanuck felt, wrongly as it turned out, that Grable would be a star for many years to come and looked on Monroe as just another starlet trying to sleep her way to the top. Also, Monroe's sex appeal was different to that of Grable's. Grable exuded a girl-next-door kind of sex, promoted cheekily at times when the studio squeezed her into a tight, one-piece white bathing suit, but a homely kind of appeal nonetheless. Zanuck knew how to handle that.

With Monroe things were different. She radiated an incandescent quality and a more obvious kind of sex. When playing comedy she also seemed to be able to

Marilyn Monroe as the seductive Rose Loomis in Henry Hathaway's torrid 1953 thriller, Niagara*, the first of Marilyn's starring films.*

kid sex rather than treat it seriously and this rather baffled the Fox executives. It was all too obvious what was up there on screen but they seemed at a loss as to how to promote it. Groucho Marx summed it up when he described Monroe as 'Mae West, Theda Bara and Bo–Peep all rolled into one'.

Monroe was finally launched when it became obvious that Grable no longer had box office appeal. The year was 1953 and Fox cast her in three films, all of them with large budgets and all of them in colour. In *Niagara*, a melodrama by Henry Hathaway, she played a treacherous, slinky *femme fatale*; in *Gentlemen Prefer Blondes* she starred as Anita Loos' dumb blonde, Lorelei Lee, and sang 'Diamonds Are A Girl's Best Friend'; and in *How To Marry A Millionaire* she joined Betty Grable and Lauren Bacall as one of the three girls searching for husbands in New York City. Just one of the films would have done the trick and made her a star; the three together turned her into a superstar.

How To Marry A Millionaire was the second CinemaScope picture to be released by Fox. Directed by Jean Negulesco it was a lightweight, but wittily scripted, concoction that required little from its performers. Marilyn, however, was determined to treat it seriously. Her drama coach, the Russian Natasha Lytess, insisted that she ask Negulesco for the motivation behind the character. When Negulesco explained in some exasperation that it was only a larkish comedy and that she was just one of three girls searching for a husband who was rich rather than poor, it didn't seem to help. When Negulesco tried again and suggested that she was the kind of girl who kept hot dogs, orchids and champagne in her ice box that still didn't settle things. At last Negulesco said. 'The motivation, Miss Monroe, is that your character is short sighted. You're as blind as a bat without your glasses. *That* is your motivation.' And that seemed to satisfy her.

Negulesco's film put the seal on Marilyn Monroe's most successful and probably happiest year in movies. She received more than 5000 fan letters a week, at least a dozen of them proposing marriage, and she occupied a dressing room formerly inhabited by Marlene Dietrich. All she needed were follow-up films to build on her phenomenal success. The films did not materialize. Instead of trying to cultivate her image and fashion scripts that would enhance and even subtlely change her new found status Fox offered her second-rate, even third-rate material.

Even during this early stage of her stardom she baulked at some of the things that were offered but she did agree to do a western with Robert Mitchum called *River Of No Return*. She said 'yes' primarily because the picture was being directed by Otto Preminger, then one of the most respected names in Hollywood. He, it turned out, was only doing it because he owed Fox a picture, so it was a mistake all round. Monroe played a saloon singer, Mitchum a widowed homesteader with a 10-year-old son. After ridding themselves of gambler Rory Calhoun and being pursued downriver by Indians they fall in love. It was as simple as that. Monroe summed it up as 'A Z cowboy movie in which the acting finishes third to the scenery and CinemaScope'. She also didn't think too highly of her other 1954 film *There's No Business Like Show Business*, a lavish tribute to Irving Berlin in

Monroe and Mitchum, and high hopes, but a box office team that didn't quite come off! River Of No Return (20th Century Fox, 1954).

which she co-starred with Ethel Merman, Dan Dailey and Donald O'Connor and wriggled about uneasily to such numbers as 'Heat Wave' and 'Lazy'.

To be fair to Fox they did have their problems. Like other Hollywood studios they had been going through a hard time financially. Television was cutting more and more into their audience and they felt compelled to come up with something new, something that people couldn't get at home in their living rooms. The CinemaScope process was their answer. It was projected onto a huge letter-box shaped screen that was $2\frac{1}{2}$ times as wide as it was high. The instructions from Zanuck were that everyone and everything had to be photographed in the process, preferably in DeLuxe colour and against the most exotic backgrounds. Zanuck, once the epitomy of intelligence and good taste (*Gentleman's Agreement, All About Eve, Viva Zapata*) ignored quality scripts and decreed that locations would be the most important things about Fox movies in the future. The stars came a close second, the writers and directors a long way back in third place. Writer Nunnally Johnson later said the only way he could write for CinemaScope was to put the paper in the typewriter sideways. The profit and loss situation was so perilous at Fox that Zanuck scarcely had time to build the career of the one new star that had emerged at the studio in the 1950s. If he'd have given the matter a little more thought he would have saved himself a lot of trouble.

Zanuck received his first refusal from Monroe in 1954 when he offered her a film called *The Girl In Pink Tights*. Her co-star was to be Frank Sinatra. Sinatra had then just won an Academy Award and was being offered $5000 a week; Monroe was on $1500. She turned it down, not only because of the inferior terms but because the film was, in her words, 'a piece of junk' She also turned down the opportunity to play an early nineteenth-century mistress in *The Girl In The Red Swing* and a prostitute in *The Revolt Of Mamie Stover*. Fox thought these were admirable roles. Monroe did not. Instead she preferred to build on her publicity by entertaining the troops in Korea and wooing, then wedding, the baseball hero Joe DiMaggio.

None of this pleased Zanuck or Fox for it kept off screen the star who was now their most valuable asset. Marilyn, upset that better offers were not coming her way left for New York. Milton Greene, a photographer for *Life* and *Look* magazines, and attorney Frank Delaney convinced her that she could do better for herself, financially and artistically, if she incorporated. They also told her that there were enough loopholes in her Fox contract to allow her to break it and take Fox to court.

At a press conference in December 1954, Marilyn announced that she had formed Marilyn Monroe Productions and that she intended to appear in several ambitious productions, among them *The Brothers Karamazov* in which she would play Grushenka. Fox countered by replying that, as far as they were concerned, Monroe was still under contract (and suspension) and that she would not be able to make pictures for anyone but them for three years and four months. 'She's under contract and she'll fulfil it', they said.

Marilyn Monroe, off set during the location filming of the CinemaScope Western River Of No Return *(1954).*

Marilyn Monroe

◄ *Marilyn Monroe as the saloon entertainer Kay Weston in Otto Preminger's* River Of No Return.

If Marilyn had not had a finished film awaiting release its more than likely that she and Fox would have been at loggerheads for months, possibly years. Luckily the film in the pipeline was a Grade A production, *The Seven Year Itch*. It had been directed by the great Billy Wilder and even though her role in the picture was still that of the dumb blonde, Marilyn had accepted it without hesitation. It was the first time that she had had the opportunity to make a film with a director of Wilder's quality. *The Seven Year Itch* was not a great film. It was not even a good film. Today, it looks more than a little laboured. But there remains something beguiling about its story of a married publisher (played by Tom Ewell) who fantasizes about the model (Monroe) who lives above him in his New York apartment. Its basic problem was that, because of the censorship of the day, audiences knew that nothing was going to happen between the publisher and the girl. And that muted the film's appeal for Wilder. He said: 'Unless the husband left alone in New York, has an affair with the girl there's nothing. But you couldn't do that in those days, so I was straightjacketed.'

Nonetheless, the success of the play on which it was based (it ran for three years on Broadway) ensured that *The Seven Year Itch* was a box office smash. During filming Wilder came face to face with Monroe's increasingly difficult behaviour on set and also her by then well-known tardiness. She wasn't the only star who liked to arrive late but, according to many directors, she was the worst. The fact that her marriage to DiMaggio was already on the rocks also didn't put her in the best frame of mind. Wilder treated her gently. He'd seen enough of Hollywood temperament to know how to handle it. He said: 'She was scared and unsure of herself, so much so that I found myself wishing that I were a psychoanalyst and she was my patient. She would have looked lovely on a couch.' He added:

> Marilyn is an extraordinarily capable natural actress. She would be the greatest if she ran like a watch. But you can never tell when or if she'll show up for work.
>
> When we filmed *The Seven Year Itch* she was never on time once. It is a terrible thing for an acting company, the director, the cameraman. You sit there and wait. You can't start without her. Thousands of dollars you see going into the hole. You can always figure a Monroe picture runs an extra few hundred thousand because she's coming late. It demoralizes the whole company. It's like trench warfare. You sit and sit, waiting for something to happen. When are the shells going to explode? On the other hand I have an Aunt Ida in Vienna who is always on time, but I wouldn't put her in a movie.

Wilder was genuinely non-plussed by Monroe's behaviour. It even gave him sleepless night trying to figure it out: 'What is it? Is she late on purpose? No. Perhaps her idea of time is deranged. You think maybe there's a little watchmaker in Zurich and he makes a living producing special watches only for Marilyn.'

Wilder eventually thought he had found the answer when he accepted a lift from her in Hollywood. He equated the state of her mind with the atrocious muddle in the back of her car.

▶ *Ecstasy! Both for Monroe and the audience as Marilyn Monroe's dress is blown high above the New York subway grating in a scene from Billy Wilder's 1955 comedy,* The Seven Year Itch.

▼ *An innocent Marilyn Monroe and an eager Tom Ewell in Billy Wilder's* The Seven Year Itch *(1955).*

Once, when my car was in overhaul she gave me a lift from Fox to my house. She was driving this black Cadillac of hers. She received it from Jack Benny. She was a guest on his television programme and it was her salary. I looked in the back of her car. Such a mess you wouldn't believe. It is like she threw everything in the back helter-skelter because there's an invasion and the enemy is already in Pasadena. There's blouses lying there, and slacks, girdles, skirts, shoes, old plane tickets, old lovers for all I know – you never saw such a filthy mess in your life.

Working with Wilder gave Monroe just the filip she needed. Due to her lateness the film came in three weeks over schedule and $1,800,000 over budget. But thanks to her performance and the publicity generated from her being photographed standing above a New York subway grating, her skirt billowing above her head because of the gusts from the trains, the picture grossed $6,000,000.

The box-office success of *The Seven Year Itch* convinced Fox to try for a compromise. In August 1955 they offered her a new contract. Marilyn would make four films for the studio in seven years but would also be allowed to make pictures outside the studio. She could, if she wished, appear in up to six television shows a year. Most important of all, she had director approval. She saw this as the best way to escape from her stereotype. By 1956 she no longer wanted to play 'dumb blondes' and resented any attempt by her studio to depict her as frivolous and foolish. She said:

I'm nobody's slave and never have been. Nobody hypnotizes me to do this or that. You never see on the screen 'This picture was directed by an ignorant director with no taste'. No, the public always blames the star. *Me*. I had directors who were so stupid all they could do was repeat the lines of the script to me like they're reading a timetable.

She added:

I want to develop. I want to grow in stature, to be a real actress. In New York I learned to make friends. Before, I never had any friends, only conquests. I didn't have the time to find real friends. I was always being looked at, I had no chance to look. I am perfectly serious about wanting to act seriously.

Ironically, it was when she decided to become a serious actress that things started to go wrong for Monroe. The new-found freedom should have allowed her to blossom and expand her talents. She certainly did all the right things. She attended the Lee Strasberg Actor's Studio in New York where she learned the 'Method' school of acting and chose as her first 'serious' film project, *Bus Stop*. The picture was based on the play by William Inge and was directed by Joshua Logan. Monroe played Cherie, a third-rate saloon singer who eventually hooks up with a naïve hot-blooded young cowboy (played by Don Murray).

Much has been made of Monroe's performance in *Bus Stop*, how moving and realistic she was and how affecting when she sang the song 'That Old Black Magic'. And there's no doubt that she did indeed bring a sensitivity and pathos to her role. But if anyone but Monroe had given the performance it's doubtful whether critics or audiences would have looked twice. Any one of a dozen

▼ A cry for help! Monroe in her first serious dramatic role as Cherie in Joshua Logan's Bus Stop *(1956).*

actresses could have played the part as well, indeed better. Those who argued that Monroe was unlucky not to receive an Oscar nomination should have looked more closely at the acting, in the same film, of Betty Field as the owner of a roadside diner. Field, a fine actress, dealt effortlessly with her role, Monroe looked what she was, an immature performer struggling desparately to be serious.

It has never been made clear, despite all the books and documentaries, whether Monroe was satisfied with her performance in *Bus Stop*. But it seems unlikely that she was impressed. If she had been, she would surely have pursued things further. But after *Bus Stop* nothing happened. All the publicity and build-up seemed to have come to nothing. It may have been that Monroe suddenly realised her limitations. Or that the filming of *Bus Stop* proved to be too much of an ordeal and that being a serious dramatic actress was harder work than she'd imagined.

On the other hand it may just have been a question of bad timing and that the turmoil of her private life got in the way of her film career at exactly the wrong moment. She met and married Arthur Miller which brought her more publicity than her performance in *Bus Stop*. She suffered subsequent miscarriages when she tried to have a child and she was in the news again when Miller had to face the House Un-American Activities Committee and refused to name those among his friends who were left wing. In June 1956 *The Daily Express* in London reported:

> One way for an actress to get herself disliked in America at this moment is for her to have any connection with Communism – even some remote 'guilt by association' is enough. Women's clubs and ex-service organisations would boycott her films. Studios discover they have no parts for her. It could happen to Marilyn Monroe

It didn't, but nothing else seemed to go right for Monroe as the 1950s drew to a close. Just when she'd won her fight with Fox and things should have been going well, life turned sour. She appeared in other films but in each of them she was once again the stereotype she had always been. She visited Britain to appear with, and be directed by, Laurence Olivier in a version of Terence Rattigan's *The Prince And The Showgirl*. She found it difficult to take direction. One morning, when she came on set, Olivier instructed her to be 'sexy'. She looked bewildered at Olivier's attempt at humour and stumbled through the scene. When Olivier tried again and suggested that, in order to calm herself, she count slowly she remained as tense as ever. 'My God she can't even count', he cried.

Marilyn's best film of the period, and some would say the best of all her films was *Some Like It Hot*, made in 1959. The director was once again Billy Wilder. After *The Seven Year Itch* he had vowed he would never work with her again. He changed his mind when Arthur Miller rang him and suggested that Marilyn appear in the film because she was depressed after a miscarriage. Wilder cast Marilyn as the dizzy dance band singer Sugar Kane who pals up with a couple of male jazz musicians when they pose as two members of an all-girls dance band travelling to Florida.

He soon realized that things were as bad as ever. Indeed, worse. The lateness had not improved. She would snarl and be unpleasant on set. When called that she was needed for a scene she would yell 'fuck you' from her dressing room. And when she was ready she would not always take to Wilder's suggestions: 'Don't talk to me now, I'm thinking about how I'm going to play this scene.'

For Wilder the making of the film was one of his unhappiest experiences. When he'd worked with her earlier she hadn't begun her classes at the Strasberg school. Then he'd argued against it:

> They're trying to elevate Marilyn to a level where she can't exist. She will lose her audience. She is a calendar girl with warmth, charm, great charm. Marilyn's whole success is she can't act. She's going through a bad evolution. If she takes it seriously it is the end of Monroe.

Four years later he backtracked. 'I was wrong', he said.

> She has become a better actress, a deeper actress, since Strasberg. But I still believe she was developing herself naturally and would have become greater even without him. I still say she was encouraged in her bad habits. Now it takes longer to get a scene done. If she were working alone, it would be all right. But she's playing with others – and she wears them out.
>
> Before she was like a tight rope walker who doesn't know there's a pit below she can fall into. Now she knows. She is more careful on the tightrope. She's more self conscious. I'm still not convinced she needed training. God gave her everything. The first day a photographer took a picture of her, she was a genius.

Tony Curtis was the actor who suffered the most on *Some Like It Hot*. A professional performer who would usually get it right within two or three takes he found that he had to go 10, 20, on one occasion 59 takes in scenes with Marilyn. The longer he went the worse he became, the longer she went the better she became. One day there was no shooting at all because of her lateness. Jack Lemmon and Curtis were scheduled for an 11.00 a.m. call, Monroe for 1.00 p.m. She arrived two and a half hours late. By the time she had been prepared for the cameras it was ten past six. When she flounced onto the stage it was deserted. Wilder had dismissed the crew at six and left himself at the same time. Each day that he did not film added at least $30,000 to the film's cost.

By the time Wilder filmed *Some Like It Hot*, Marilyn Monroe was drinking heavily and walking around for much of the time like a zombie. Nembutal sleeping pills left her incapacitated for much of the time. Sometimes she would be made-up whilst lying flat in bed. On other occasions she would vomit, pass out or become too dizzy to act. She would blow even the simplest of lines. In one scene she had to enter a room in which Lemmon and Curtis are in their dresses and ask, 'Where's the bourbon?' Then she had to open and close drawers looking for an enema bag containing whisky. The line proved impossible to say. She would either say, 'Where's the whisky?' or, 'Where's the bonbon?' or, 'Where's the bottle?' In the end the only way she could get it right was by reading it from strips of paper that Wilder had pasted in every drawer of the bureau. Wilder was utterly dependent on her moods. In some cases he had to match shots from different takes to make it seem as though Marilyn was giving a performance. Jack Lemmon looked on her plight with sympathy:

> She was a sweet lady who was clearly going through some kind of hell on earth. I didn't know all the reasons but I saw she was suffering – suffering and still producing that magic on film. It was a courageous performance, really courageous. Most actors only occasionally use all their talent but Marilyn was using hers constantly, giving everything she had, till it hurt

Once Billy Wilder had finished shooting *Some Like It Hot* he let it be known that his health had improved greatly since the completion of the picture: 'I am eating better. My back doesn't ache anymore. I am able to sleep for the first time in months. And I can look at my wife without wanting to hit her because she's a woman.' Asked whether he would ever consider working with Marilyn again, he replied: 'I have discussed this with my doctor and my psychiatrist and my accountant and they tell me I'm too old and too rich to go through this again.'

Yet, when he bought the rights to *Irma La Douce* he did admit that he was considering using her for a third time. When he told this to Art Buchwald in Paris in the summer of 1960 Buchwald reminded him of the long hours he'd had to wait on set for Marilyn to turn up and how frustrating that had been. Wilder replied:

> But we didn't waste those hours. We played poker, I managed to read *War and Peace, Les Miserables* and *Hawaii*, and we all got wonderful sun-tans. The extras made twice as much money as they expected, and while it may have taken slightly longer to make the film, we did get to know each other so much better.

Wilder again had an answer when Buchwald reminded him of Marilyn's inability to learn her lines. He said: 'That's the beauty of working with Monroe. She's not a parrot. Anyone can remember lines, but it takes a real artist to come on the set and not know her lines and give the performance she did.' He added that if he did decide to use Marilyn in the part and made the picture in Paris they wouldn't be wasting their time because if she did show up late on set they could all learn to paint.

Marilyn was furious when she read these remarks. She never saw Wilder again. Ironically, he was in Paris shooting location sequences for *Irma La Douce* when she died. Several years later he told a journalist in the Los Angeles Times:

> Marilyn was mean. Terribly mean. The meanest woman I have ever met around this town. I am appalled by this cult that has grown up. It's getting to be an act of

Marilyn Monroe

Monroe before the cameras for the last time. A test shot for the ill-fated Something's Gotta Give.

courage to say anything but saintly things about her. Well, let me be courageous. I have never met anyone as utterly mean as Marilyn Monroe – nor as utterly fabulous on the screen, and that includes Garbo.

In 1985 he confessed to missing her: 'In the last fifteen years there were ten projects that came to me, and I'd start working on them and I'd think, "It's not going to work, it needs Marilyn Monroe". Nobody else is in that orbit; everyone else is earthbound by comparison.'

There have been many theories as to why Marilyn Monroe destroyed herself. Some said that she was afraid of growing old and that was why she tried to become a serious actress, as some kind of insurance against finishing up as a Garbo-like recluse in a Beverly Hills mansion. Others said that she couldn't face up to the fact that she simply wasn't good enough as a dramatic actress. Joseph Cotten, her co-star in *Niagara*, remembered that although she had a buoyancy of spirit she was 'cursed with less than her share of confidence and more of her share of insecurity, both dark synonyms of fear' She would, he said, 'move into outer space and into a cloud of blackness.'

By the time she came to make John Huston's *The Misfits*, the story of a group of modern-day cowboys and a frightened divorcee in Reno, Nevada, her marriage to Arthur Miller was all but over and her big problem was lack of sleep. Huston said:

> She was in very bad shape. She was really in no condition to do the picture. She shouldn't have been anywhere near the camera if truth be known. She had this terrible worry about sleeping. She had by then become reliant on pills. She needed them to put her to sleep and then to wake her up again.

Huston was so disturbed by Marilyn's actions and appearance that he took Arthur Miller to one side and pleaded with him to get her off the drugs. He told him that if she didn't stop she would be in an institution in two or three years – or dead. Miller looked at Huston and gave a hopeless gesture. He'd been through it all, many times. There was nothing he could do. He was at the end of his rope.

Halfway through the production Marilyn broke down completely and was sent to Los Angeles for hospitalization for two weeks. The production closed down but everyone including the all-star cast, (Clark Gable, Montgomery Clift, Eli Wallach), had to be paid in full. When she arrived back on location in Nevada, Huston went to visit her at her hotel to get some idea of what he could expect on the set in the week ahead. He found that Miller had moved to another hotel and that Monroe showed little sign of improvement:

> She greeted me enthusiastically to start with then went into a kind of trance. She was the worst I'd ever seen her. Her hair was a tangle; her hands and feet were grubby; she was wearing only a short nightgown which wasn't any cleaner than the rest of her. There was something touching about her then, a kind of vulnerability. I knew somehow – we all did – that something awful was going to happen to her.

The Misfits was the last film that Marilyn Monroe completed. At Fox she began the comedy *Something's Gotta Give*. Out of 32 days shooting she turned up on just 12 occasions and then rarely in a suitable condition. The studio which was

then reeling from the huge cost of the epic *Cleopatra* was not prepared to indulge her any more and fired her. At the same time they handed her a $750,000 lawsuit for losses caused to the studio. Two months later she was found dead in her Hollywood home by her housekeeper. She was nude and lying face down. One hand touched a telephone, the other clutched a sheet to her throat. An empty bottle of sedatives was found close by.

Since her death there have been rumours that she did not commit suicide, that is was an accident, that she was involved with the Mafia, and also with the two Kennedy brothers, John and Bobby. Documentaries have been made and books written to prove that there were murder plots, that she 'knew too much' about some political scandal, that there was great significance that she skipped shooting on *Something's Gotta Give* to sing at President Kennedy's birthday party. But all the evidence, such as it is, has been circumstantial.

The truth about Monroe is almost certainly much simpler than the theorists would have us believe. She was an actress who lived out her dreams in a make believe world, trying to forget her past. She had a limited talent that was instinctive. She couldn't (or refused to) recognize her limitations and tried to stretch further than she could. When she found that she could not reach, she stumbled and found that going back to being a sex symbol was not enough.

In the 1950s she delighted in and then fought against the image of the luscious, undulating, brainless female. She was made to become part of that image and as the image grew into a symbol found it difficult to prevent herself and her own life from being absorbed and merged with her on-screen personality. In the end she was a lost soul.

When she died it was thought her estate would be worth a million dollars. But she was broke. She owed $917,000 in back taxes and it was not until 1969 that an upswing in residual payments offset the deficit. Just before she died she gave an interview to *Life* magazine about the film *Something's Gotta Give*. The magazine carried stills of her bathing nude in an indoor swimming pool. She looked slim and attractive. One of the remarks she made during the interview was:

> It might be some kind of relief to be finished. It's sort of like, I don't know, what kind of a yard you're running, but then you're at the finishing line and you sort of sigh – you've made it. But you never have – you have to start all over again.

It was a sad little comment made by a tired woman of 36 who seemed to have run her course and was only too aware of it.

On the other hand if you ask a Los Angeles taxi driver about Marilyn's final words he'll give you a different version – and almost certainly one with a happy ending.

8. George Sanders

George Sanders

Many take issue with the claim that George Sanders was a star. He was, they argue, more a character actor, a man with an urbane charm and a unique personality but hardly to be compared with the likes of Tracy or Gable or Flynn. And to a certain extent they have a point, but for a while in the 1940s George Sanders did have his following and for a year or two looked as though he might actually emerge as one of the most distinctive actors of his generation.

That he didn't finally make it was due to his own lack of confidence, a dearth of well-written roles that would have accommodated his haughty, cynical persona, and because, very early on in his career, George Sanders simply gave up. Within a few months of arriving in Hollywood he judged that to become and remain a star he needed to work hard, be under constant pressure and enjoy more than a fair share of luck. He decided that the odds were too heavily stacked against him and opted instead for a calmer, somewhat saner existence. On screen he allowed himself to be extended only infrequently. He later excused his attitude by saying: 'I am not one of those people who would rather act than eat. Larry Olivier was born with the desire to act. I was not. My own desire as a boy was to retire. The ambition has never changed.'

Sanders delighted in making such remarks throughout his thirty-five year career. Those close to him knew that for most of the time they served as a front for his fear of failure, that he used them to cushion his very real misgivings about his own limited talent. Even if he had tried for stardom he doubted that he would have made it so he opted to play himself as often as he could. The public loved him for it. They revelled in his superior cads, his world-weary cynicism and his elegant fatalism. To listen to George Sanders dismiss a woman with a wave of his hand and a stinging riposte was one of the cinematic delights of the 1940s and 1950s.

But it wasn't so much the stature of his screen performances that made George Sanders a star. It was his life off-screen that earned him his reputation. In public he played George Sanders to the hilt, carrying around with him an air of sophisticated romance, total indifference and a take-it-or-leave-it philosophy that women found difficult to resist. He cultivated the role of the professional cynic and would drop barbed epigrams to any journalist who happened to be around: 'While love may turn a man into a poet it is more likely to turn him into a bore', he said. And again: 'Women never need to bait the male...man is trapped from the start.'

Sanders realised quite early on that he had a quite unique image and that a facade rather than talent was all that was required to succeed in the shallow world of films. He didn't really need his pictures, other than for the money they brought him and which he enjoyed spending. Being himself was enough. With his cool mocking eyes and scornful manner he meticulously built a cad's exterior to shock the world and for more than thirty years was the personification of the man about town. He was one of the first movie stars to become a name through his personality rather than through his films. And in that respect he has a rather special place in Hollywood history.

George Sanders

He arrived in Hollywood after a brief career in musicals on the London stage and appearing in a handful of British films. He was born in St Petersburg in 1906; his father was a rope manufacturer, and his mother a British horticulturist. He escaped from Russia with his family during the Revolution and came to England where he was educated first at Brighton College and then at Manchester Technical College. He spent some time in the textile business and in a tobacco enterprise in South America before drifting into a career on stage. He played smallish parts in the 1920s and 1930s, earning a reputation for light comedy and his musical talents. He made his screen debut in 1936 in *Find The Lady*.

His first American film, the historical epic *Lloyds of London*, quickly established him in the kind of role he would be required to play in the years that lay ahead – that of a villainous, superior aristocrat who finally perishes in a duel, at the hands of the film's hero Tyrone Power. If Sanders had entertained any hopes that he might himself become a romantic lead, they were quickly dispelled with *Lloyds Of London*. He was only thirty-one and a tall (6 ft 3 in), imposing figure of a man, but compared with Power he was very far from what Hollywood producers required as a leading man.

Nonetheless he quickly found a niche for himself as the English bounder of the public school variety, the kind who although charming was not entirely trustworthy and would utter a lazy 'old boy' every other sentence. When those roles dried up for a while Hollywood would crop his hair, give him a monocle and a pair of tight shining boots and cast him at the opposite end of the spectrum as the perfect Nazi.

Sanders wavered uncertainly between these two stereotypes for most of his early years in Hollywood. He also played Leslie Charteris's smooth adventurer 'The Saint' in a series of B-movies at RKO and then another amateur detective 'The Falcon' at the same studio. When he was criticized by those who thought he should be doing rather better for himself he replied: 'I make no pretence. I play myself quite beautifully. It's not tiring for me to do that. I learn my lines when required, sometimes I even speak them.'

He also found a convincing excuse for turning his back on stardom. He said:

> Had I become a big time romantic star I might now be a good deal richer than I am; on the other hand it is quite conceivable that I would no longer be around professionally speaking; the mortality rate among stars is extremely high whereas a good character actor is almost indestructible. Even with one foot in the grave it is possible for such an actor to go on earning a good living, since there seem to be a large number of parts which required actors to look half dead; and in fact these circumstances may lend a verisimilitude to his performance which his acting never could.

Sanders' brilliant use of the English language whenever he commented on his life and screen career should have persuaded writers in Hollywood to write specially for him. Ernst Lubitsch and Billy Wilder would have been ideal directors to guide him through polished and sophisticated comedies. But the chance to work with them never came Sanders' way.

◀ *George Sanders as the decadent Lord Henry Wotton in Albert Lewin's 1945 version of* The Picture of Dorian Gray.

▼ *George Sanders (fourth from left) pictured with (left to right) C. Aubrey Smith, Laurence Olivier, Joan Fontaine and Judith Anderson in Alfred Hitchcock's* Rebecca *(1940).*

Hitchcock though found a use for him in a couple of films – *Foreign Correspondent* and *Rebecca* (he was a public school type in both) – as did Albert Lewin when he cast him as the Gauguin-styled painter Howard Strickland in a version of Somerset Maugham's *The Moon And Sixpence*. But the two films that really established him as an actor to be reckoned with were *The Picture Of Dorian Gray* (again directed by Lewin, in 1945) in which he was perfectly cast as Oscar Wilde's decadent aristocrat Lord Henry Wotton, and *All About Eve*, made five years later. In the latter film he played the acid-tongued drama critic Addison DeWitt. He gave a devastating performance, one that earned him an Academy Award as the best supporting actor of the year. His writer and director was Joseph L. Mankiewicz and even Sanders expressed satisfaction with his portrayal.

George Sanders as New York theatre critic Addison DeWitt, his Oscar-winning role in All About Eve *(1950).*

The film was about the skullduggery and machinations that go on behind the scenes on Broadway. Bette Davis played an ageing star, Anne Baxter her scheming understudy and Sanders the critic who wryly observes all the treachery unfolding in front of him. *All About Eve* won six Oscars including best picture but it was not a big moneymaker. And that in no way surprised Sanders. He said:

Our film was frequently brilliant and sophisticated. What it lacked was the necessary basic formula of the 40s and 50s which, when brought down to its basics, was boy meets girl, boy loses girl, boy gets girl back again. Within this framework it is permissible to do all sorts of things – one can be witty, daring, original, profound or even dull. One has a great deal of lassitude. The boy, for instance, can be a dipsomaniac and the girl can be a misguided member of the Ku Klux Klan, as long as they meet, part and get together again. Or the boy can be a Martian and the girl a Mormon. The permutations are infinite. In the case of *All About Eve* there was no such appeal to the basic emotions. Our film was about sophisticated, ambitious, wickedly amusing people. The audience wasn't rooting for any of us.

▲ All About Eve (1950), winner of six Acadamy Awards. Left to right; Bette Davis, Gary Merrill, Anne Baxter and George Sanders.

The Oscar for *All About Eve* made little difference to Sanders' career. He really hadn't expected that it would although he had hoped that it might have resulted in him being able to negotiate more rewarding terms. He was wrong. He gave a passable imitation of himself (as the owner of a department store) in *I Can Get It For You Wholesale*, a drama of the rag trade starring Susan Hayward, and director Richard Brooks offered him a few worthwhile lines as a smooth art crook in *The Light Touch*. But the pickings were generally meagre. Apart from the lavish musical *Call Me Madam* in which he was able to use his singing voice for the first time in a Hollywood film it was mostly dross. The other exceptions, rather surprisingly, were historical epics to which, for some reason, Hollywood producers thought him ideally suited. De Mille, for instance, cast him as the Saran of Gaza who lusts after Hedy Lamarr in *Samson And Delilah*, MGM gave him a mace and sword and told him to despatch Robert Taylor in *Ivanhoe* and King Vidor cast him as the villain in the large scale but ill-fated epic *Solomon And Sheba*.

◀ (left) *A beautiful Hedy Lamarr and a pensive George Sanders, beautifully costumed by Edith Head in Cecil B. De Mille's 1950 spectacular* Samson and Delilah.

◀ (right) *Ethel Merman as 'The Hostess with the Mostess' with a musical George Sanders in Walter Lang's 1953 version of Irving Berlin's Broadway hit,* Call Me Madam.

Tyrone Power and Gina Lollobrigida had the starring roles in *Solomon And Sheba* which was shot in Spain in the autumn of 1958. Over the years Power and Sanders had become friends. They had made several pictures together, all of them costume dramas – *Lloyds Of London, The Black Swan, Son Of Fury*. In most, Sanders had perished in the last reel after a long and arduous duel. In *Solomon And Sheba* the situation was much as before. Power versus Sanders with poor George expiring after his double had exerted himself on his behalf. But on Saturday the fifteenth of November the roles were tragically reversed and for real.

The day's shooting call included Power, Sanders and the two doubles. The stars rehearsed the scene under the guidance of King Vidor and then wandered to their respective trailers while the cameraman and his assistants lit the set. After a while, Sanders began to wonder about the length of the delay. Tyrone Power wasn't feeling too well he was told. Something to do with a spasm. He should be alright in about half an hour.

George Sanders

Sanders, who remembered Power having said that he had a touch of bursitis, looked in through the door of Power's trailer and asked if he could do anything to help. Power was sitting in a chair. He was twisted over on his left side and holding on tightly to his arm. His neck was tilted over rigidly. Power told him that it was the bursitis again and tried to laugh it off. Sanders got no further as the producer Ted Richmond came in looking more than a little concerned. Several minutes later they decided that they couldn't wait for the doctor who was supposedly on his way. Power was carried to Lollobrigida's Mercedes which was near the dressing-room trailer. The car went at top speed through the streets of Madrid. The nearest hospital was twelve minutes away. Three minutes into the trip Power died. Sanders who had been fencing with him just half an hour before, was the last man to appear with him in front of the cameras. He was shaken and disturbed. Power had become one of his closest friends in the film business and just the night before the two of them had been discussing their plans about settling in Switzerland. A few days later Sanders revealed a warmer, more compassionate side to his nature when he delivered an eloquent eulogy:

I shall always remember Tyrone Power as a bountiful man. A man who gave freely of himself. It mattered not to whom he gave. His concern was in the giving.

I shall always remember his wonderful smile. A smile that would light up the darkest hour of the day like a sunburst.

I shall always remember Tyrone Power as a man who gave more of himself than it was wise for him to give. Until in the end he gave his life.

Sanders, like most of the others in the cast, would have preferred to have forgotten all about *Solomon And Sheba* after Power's death. Nearly three-quarters of the picture had been shot but not enough to complete it without hiring another star to replace Power who still had many scenes to film. Yul Brynner was brought in as a replacement which meant that Sanders had to refilm all those scenes he had already played with Power. It was a depressing experience especially when he had to re-enact the duelling scene. Sanders cynicism later returned when he described Brynner's arrival on the set. He said:

Brynner brought with him an entourage of seven, the function of one member of the retinue consisting entirely of placing already lighted cigarettes in Brynner's outstretched fingers. Another was permanently occupied in shaving Brynner's skull with an electric razor whenever the suspicion of a shadow darkened the noble head. While these services were being rendered unto him Brynner sat in sphinx-like splendour wearing black leather suits or white leather suits of which he had half a dozen each, confected for him by the firm of Dior.

I never discovered what were the duties of the remaining five members of his staff but they were no doubt doing work that was equally essential. I must admit that I have never felt unduly hard done by because I have had to light my own cigarettes – still I was impressed. I came to the conclusion that Brynner was a very shrewd fellow; he has one intense expression which he uses all the time on screen and one intense expression is more valuable to a film star than a dozen faces.

And that's the important thing for a film star, to have an interesting face. He doesn't have to move it very much. Editing and camerawork can always produce the desired illusion that an acting performance is being given.

A bearded and unrecognizable George Sanders duels with Tyrone Power in the 1942 swashbuckler The Black Swan.

▶ *Tyrone Power (back to camera) faces up to George Sanders in King Vidor's 1958 epic* Solomon and Sheba. *Power died shortly after this photograph was taken.*

▶ Solomon and Sheba. *Same battle, different star: George Sanders perishes at the hands of Power's replacement, Yul Brynner.*

What Sanders failed to mention in that typically cynical dismissal of his craft was the use by the actor of the voice. And here he was supreme. His mocking tones were like those of no other screen actor. He could be utterly charming but he could also extract the very last drop from an insult. Few actors could match him, except perhaps Claude Rains. He may indeed have cultivated just the one expression – the haughty sneer – but when he embellished that with an impeccable delivery the effect was mesmerizing.

Sanders' private life during the 1950s and 1960s was, as always, never far from the headlines. Not without initiative when it came to trying to make money outside of acting he once rang James Mason, who in 1948 had newly arrived in Hollywood, about a scheme to build bungalows for wealthy widows in Beverly Hills. Mason had been trained as an architect as a young man and Sanders felt that together they might make a killing, either under the name of Sanders-Mason or Mason-Sanders. But after some initial enthusiasm nothing came of the idea. Later, he became one of the directors of Cadco Developments Ltd (of all things a piggery firm!) which in 1964 eventually folded leaving him bankrupt and with debts of more than £160,000. His venture into television wasn't entirely successful either. His *George Sanders Mystery Theatre* in which he acted as host to some routine dramas ended after just a few weeks.

Neither did he enjoy much luck when he tried marriage. He enjoyed (or endured) four marriages all told including a much-publicized one to Zsa Zsa Gabor (and a subsequent one to her sister Magda). They left him rueful and wiser. 'The answer to bachelordom is not a wife but a good butler,' he said. Then, 'Marriage is a most unnatural relationship, almost invariably entered into for the wrong reasons.'

He shared a $90,000, 14-bedroom mansion with Zsa Zsa in Beverly Hills and later commented: 'I lived there as a sort of paying guest.' She thought the marriage might have worked if George had loved her as much as he loved himself. George for his part, felt that some good had come out of the union: 'Zsa Zsa introduced me to her psychiatrist and he cured me of Zsa Zsa.'

George Sanders

David Niven recalled that the only time he ever saw Sanders really worried was when he was about to get his divorce from Zsa Zsa. He realized that under the California divorce laws he could be liable for a large cash settlement if he were found to be the guilty party so he determined to obtain evidence to prove otherwise. One night he crept towards their house with a photographer armed with a ladder and a brick. The brick was to hurl through the bedroom window so that the photographer could catch Zsa Zsa and her then lover, Profiro Rubirosa in bed together. It was not needed. Zsa Zsa and Rubirosa had forgotten to lock the French windows.

Niven also remembered that Sanders was close to being the laziest person he had ever met. He never took exercise and would throw up his hands in horror at the thought of a walk along the beach or the suggestion that he might actually participate in a game of tennis or golf. Niven said:

> His reaction to war service was one of instant repulsion and he never modified it. 'The stupidest thing young men can do is to throw away their youth; as Thomas Carlyle said, "With clenched teeth and hell fire eyes hacking one another's flesh" . . . they'll never get me to do it.' And they never did . . . 'I shall keep ahead of the Sheriff', he announced. 'Luckily I hold three passports – Russian, American and British. I shall play one off against the other till they either give up or order me to do something. Then I shall immediately become a Quaker and if they tell me to drive an ambulance, I shall crash so many learning how to drive that they'll send me home.'

In the 1960s Sanders preferred to reserve his best performances for the journalists who interviewed him. He liked it best when they paid for the lunch and it was not on him. Then, as always, he was good value, regaling the lucky scribe with his views on anything from films and women to politicians and Hollywood. Always he was good copy; always he was worth the price of a meal.

He said: 'I hate to give autographs and never do. I am always rude to people. I am not a sweet person. I am not a disagreeable person. I am a hateful person. I like to be hateful.' He was of course playing the same game he had been playing for twenty years or more, the 'keep my name in the papers' game because the films he was making at the time were either fifth rate or downright lousy. He never failed to keep up his vitriolic attack on women: 'All women are liars', he would claim. 'Treat a woman badly and they'll come running. If you want to really test the strength of a woman's sex appeal then tell her to wear no make up, put her in an unflattering dress and then see if she's interesting. If she is she has charm.'

It was only when he grew older that Sanders' cynicism began to take on a more tragic tone. His bankruptcy after the Cadco debacle hit him hard and he was forced to accept just about any kind of role to pay off the debt, even appearing in British films opposite Tony Hancock and Charlie Drake. He kept himself busy to combat his loneliness but all the time his hunt for solace became more urgent. As one journalist so astutely commented: 'suddenly, behind the wisecrack lay the crack of age'.

George Sanders

George Sanders in Hollywood in the mid-1950s.

When the 1960s got into full swing and films demanded new, working class heroes and villains, Sanders suddenly found himself out of fashion. Cads, no matter how polished, were no longer interesting figures.

The market in charm had become thin. The occasional worthwhile movie would still come along: *Village Of The Damned*, a version of John Wyndham's novel *The Midwich Cuckoos; A Shot In The Dark*, the second Inspector Clouseau film to star Peter Sellers; the John Huston thriller, *The Kremlin Letter* (in which he played a homosexual spy with a penchant for drag); and Disney's *The Jungle Book* in which he was splendid as the voice of the tiger Shere Khan. But mostly it was poor stuff. The majority of his films were made in Britain or Europe. In time he came to dislike Hollywood:

> Los Angeles has changed. One thousand people a day are pouring in with a corresponding increase in motor cars. And thousands of motor cars belching carbon monoxide into the inverted atmosphere hardly produces Chanel No. 5.
>
> They estimate that to live there and to breathe that smog is equivalent to smoking two packs of cigarettes a day. I prefer to live in Majorca and actually smoke them. That way I'll be as well off as a non-smoker living in Los Angeles.

If anything Sanders became even more sardonic in his sixties. He also found a new target for his barbs – old age. He became quite obsessed with it. He said: 'There are far too many old people about. At an agreed age, say 70, they should be given a cup of hemlock and bow out.' He also disliked all those who were getting old and failed to admit to the fact. Like the American comedian George Jessel:

> The whole business of trying to look younger is repugnant. Apart from anything else, if you look young, people expect you to behave young which is terribly tiring. George Jessel has two toupees, one with long hair, one with short. When he is wearing the long haired one he will finger it and say: 'It's about time I got a haircut.' Next day, there he is wearing the short one.

Sanders was never more amusing about the subject of old age than when discussing his own family, many of whom had turned out to be long-livers. He said:

> My father lasted until he was 92. The last ten years were of no use to him at all. He was no more than a vegetable. The fact that his nanny lived to be 101 was also of little comfort to him. She hardly spoke at all. She would just mumble. And she would mumble in Latvian which was even worse. Mind you, even when she could talk she didn't say anything that was very interesting so it really didn't matter in her case.
>
> There should be voluntary euthanasia. Old people are so worthless, there's no room for them in this world. What use are they? And if you go you should go out in style, with a whole load of greedy relatives round your bed, all of whom have just been cut from the will as you breathe your last. What style, what a way to go.

Sanders would then add: 'I intend to go at 70. After that I'll be no use to anyone anymore. What a bore to have to endure me for all that length of time.'

George Sanders told journalists of his plans so often that in the end, none of

John Huston's bizarre 1970 thriller, The Kremlin Letter. Intelligence officer Patrick O'Neal with George Sanders as the nightclub drag queen, 'The Warlock'.

them took him seriously anymore. When next they saw him they would greet him with, 'Still here, George'.

When, on 26 April 1972, the news came through of his death by suicide the journalists were shocked. Few people who state publicly that they intend to end their lives actually carry out the threat. George Sanders was as good as his word.

Unfortunately, he did not go out in style or in the grandiose manner he had often talked about. Instead, he died in a small Spanish resort hotel. He had been drunk at the time and taken five tubes of Nembutal. The previous day he had been filming for Spanish TV. Those who saw him said they were certain he had lost the will to live. He was found naked in his bed. He left a note that was neither funny nor witty but desperate and sad. It read: 'Dear World, I am leaving

George Sanders, aged 65, in a scene from one of his final films, Endless Night, *released in 1971.*

because I am bored. I feel I have lived long enough. I am leaving you with your worries in this sweet cesspool. Good Luck.' He was 65.

When George Sanders died, the world of films was very different from the one he had been so much a part of for over 35 years. Four letter words had begun to work their way into what passed as screenplays. Sanders would never have been at home with such scripts. He did not belong in the modern cinema. Worse, there was no longer any room for his off-screen exploits. They were no longer newsworthy. He was, as one obituary put it, 'The Last Of The Ladykillers'. He made over 100 films. In all but a handful he played the villain – the man who stole another man's wife, escaped with the money, betrayed his best friend or achieved all three simultaneously. His heavies were so villainous, such an artful blend of charm and cruelty, that they were practically the prototype for the evil-

doer who masks his motives under a cool exterior.

He never became an addict or an alcoholic, like so many in Hollywood, perhaps because he was intelligent enough to see, at a very early age, that the film world was a sham. His witty and candid autobiography *Memoirs Of A Professional Cad* revealed him to be a splendid writer and indicated that, had he had the inclination to turn his talents to screenwriting he might have found work in that quarter.

In his youth he had been talented in many directions. Languages came easily to him – French, German, Spanish. He was a fine boxer and swimmer. He had a beautiful voice. He was musical and could play the guitar, piano and saxophone. Yet he let all that go to become something he never really wanted to be. 'I am content with mediocrity', he used to say. 'I am a highly paid slave and know that I will never become a master. To be a master you need to have a personality totally different than mine.'

Three years before he died he said:

> I'm a cynic. Our values are all false and life is simply a matter of pretence. The whole world is a sham. It's just boring. I don't know where society is going and I don't care. I'm just happy I won't be around to see it. I have no friends, no interests, no plans.

Sanders was either totally honest with himself or he never gave himself a chance. Those who knew him well felt that the latter was nearer the truth. One senses, however, that Sanders was too intelligent a man to have fooled himself completely. He looked through a glass darkly with a cynical, sardonic, logical eye. He saw the film business for what it was and laughed at its pretensions; he saw himself clearly for what he was (at least in his view), an actor being paid handsome money for appearing before the cameras in a long series of mediocre films. And he saw life too starkly to endure it any longer than he had to.

9. Erich von Stroheim

Erich von Stroheim

If you check through the film reference books you'll find that nearly all the key dates in Hollywood history can be found within their pages: October 1927 when the first talkie, *The Jazz Singer*, was released; June 1935, the premiere of the first three-colour Technicolor feature *Becky Sharp*; December 1937, the release of Disney's *Snow White And The Seven Dwarfs*. But there's always one date that authors consistently overlook and that's surprising for, in many ways, it remains the most important date of all.

The date in question was 6 October 1922. It was then, at eight o'clock in the evening, that Erich von Stroheim was called from the set and brought face to face with Universal's young production head, Irving G. Thalberg. The two men stared at each other for a few seconds then Thalberg said: 'Von, you're off the picture!' By all accounts Thalberg uttered no more than those five words. Von Stroheim said none at all. He simply glared at Thalberg, turned on his heel and, with his contemptuous Prussian air, walked from the dimly lit executive suite. He never returned. For five weeks he had been working on a film called *Merry-Go-Round* He had spent a quarter of a million dollars and had little to show for it. Thalberg and the Universal studio boss, Carl Laemmle decided that they would lose money if they allowed von Stroheim to continue. Rupert Julian, a more 'reliable' director was hired to finish the picture.

The importance of 6 October 1922 was not so much that von Stroheim had been fired; it was that, for the first time, the power of a great director in the American cinema had been broken by a producer. When they heard the news, Hollywood's directors, young and old, reacted with dismay. Lewis Milestone, who later went on to direct the Oscar-winning *All Quiet On The Western Front* remembered how he felt when he learned that von Stroheim had been fired:

> It was the end of the reign of the director . . . The storm grew fiercer and when the storm subsided there was no D.W. Griffith, no James Cruze, no Rex Ingram, no Marshall Neilan. These men knew only one way of working – the way of the director: select the story, have a hand in the writing of the story, cast it, cut it, etc. When they were deprived of that method they couldn't function. They were forced to go, and they went.

Milestone, of course, was referring to the great silent directors, not the everyday workmen who churned out four, sometimes five pictures a year. Griffith, Ingram and company, through their talent and genius, had set themselves up as craftsmen who made pictures their way and who had no intention of being dictated to by producers and studio production heads whom they regarded as no more than businessmen. Thalberg was determined to change that and restrict their power. Like others in Hollywood he felt that the studios needed to be run on more profitable lines, that *they* and not the directors should choose the subjects, assign the writer and have the right to the final cut. There was a place for genius but that genius needed to be controlled and harnessed to the studio assembly line. Griffith and Ingram and von Stroheim and others would need to become part of that assembly line if they were to survive.

Erich von Stroheim

On that October night in 1922, von Stroheim became the first major director to suffer the indignity of being taken off a film. By then he had established himself as one of the top five directors working in Hollywood. There were those who ranked him even above Griffith. When he was fired from *Merry-Go-Round* he had made three films, all of them for Universal. Seduction, intrigue and a refreshingly honest look at sex were the key ingredients of his pictures, all of which were set against European backgrounds – Austria, Paris, the Riviera. If there was room for an extra helping of eroticism, debauchery and the occasional orgy or two, then so much the better. Always, von Stroheim's films probed beneath the surface, stripping away all human pretensions and mocking, often quite callously, the frailties of human nature. His films were bold and uncompromising. They were also directed and edited with great skill.

Von Stroheim acted in them whenever he could, usually as a lecherous Prussian officer who seduces the bored wife of a neglectful husband. With his immaculate dress – silk gloves, gleaming boots, cigarette holder – and his cruel, autocratic manner he quickly established himself as 'The Man You Love To Hate'.

The son of a Viennese hatter, he adopted the style of an *émigré* aristocrat when he entered films as an actor in 1914. He played minor roles and German villains throughout the duration of the war, then worked in a variety of capacities – military adviser, art director, assistant director, actor – for D.W. Griffith on *Birth Of A Nation*. It was during his period on this film that he managed to study Griffith at close quarters and first felt the desire to become a director and make his own films.

He bluffed his way into directing. After nine months of inactivity at the end of the war he presented Universal boss Carl Laemmle with a one-page outline for a film about a ruthless wife seducer in post-war Europe. Laemmle agreed. The film was called *Blind Husbands*. It was shot quickly and efficiently and made money. Von Stroheim served up similar ingredients in a second film (in which he did not star) called *The Devil's Pass Key*. Again the film was brought in on time and made a profit. It was only when he came to make his third film, *Foolish Wives*, that Laemmle and the young Thalberg realised that in von Stroheim they had employed a monster who could not be controlled. Most of the great silent directors, even if they were a law unto themselves, did at least know roughly how much they could spend and how much they could safely go over budget if needs be. Not von Stroheim. His first two Universal features turned out to have been little more than pictures on which he'd learned his craft. His third turned out to be the genuine von Stroheim. His extravagance was unleashed and never again was he able to keep it under control.

Foolish Wives was the story of a bogus nobleman who earns his living by seducing and then blackmailing rich women living on the Riviera. Von Stroheim insisted that he needed the largest sets to do full justice to the story. He built a full-scale replica of the central plaza of Monte Carlo with its Casino, the Hotel De Paris and the huge cafe. He shot for almost a year. From the initial budget of $250,000, costs rose to over a million dollars. Von Stroheim held back on

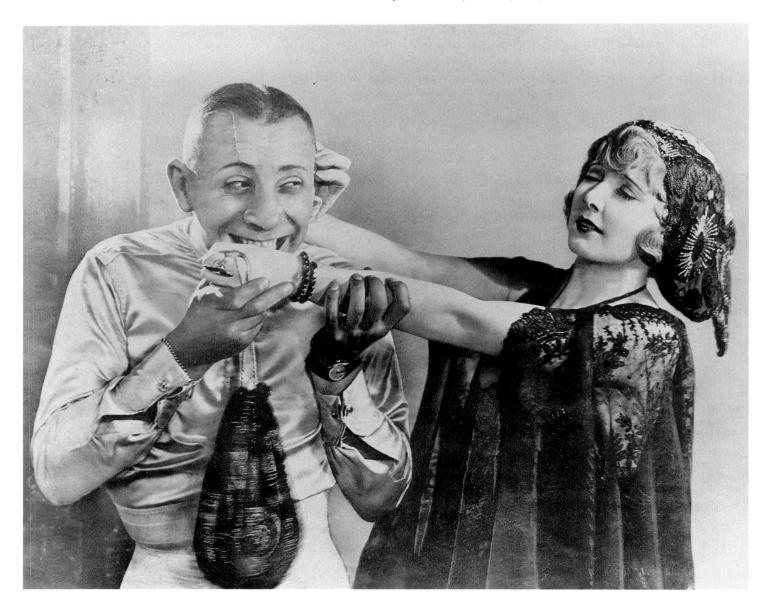

Foolish Wives (1922): Mae Busch on the receiving end of (or enjoying?) some Stroheim sadism.

nothing. He used real food and real liquor on the set even when no-one ate or drank. If the scene had to be filmed several times (as it frequently was) then the food and liquor was replaced lest it should appear cold and flat.

Expensive excursions were made for important coastal scenes. Von Stroheim filmed at the Exposition grounds at San Diego, the cliffs of La Jolla (where he shot a spectacular dive into the sea) and in the lake of a Los Angeles park for carnival night scenes. Easily his most extravagant gesture was his insistence on erecting the facades of the Riviera buildings 30 miles away at the fashionable seaside resort of Del Monte. Sometimes the weather was so bad that von Stroheim could film for only half a day. Every day the costs mounted.

Erich von Stroheim

Laemmle, realizing that it was too late to curb von Stroheim's seemingly inexhaustible appetite for perfection, finally threw in the towel and decided to advertise that *Foolish Wives* was going to be the most expensive picture made up until that time. 'The First Million Dollar Picture' claimed the advertisements, more in desperation than with pride.

Unfortunately, as was to prove the case with many of von Stroheim's pictures, a great deal of that money finished up on the cutting room floor. Von Stroheim had shot 326,000 feet of film and then edited that down to what he felt was a reasonable 32 reels. Von Stroheim let it be known that he felt his 6-hour film should be shown in two parts. Films were being shown in such a way in Europe. Why not in the States? Universal, only too well aware that a film of that length and made at such a prohibitive cost would be a financial disaster with only limited showings, decided to reduce the film. They first offered von Stroheim the job. He would have nothing to do with it, so they took the film, reduced it to a manageable 14 reels and released it to great financial success even though the profit margins were limited because of the enormous budget. Von Stroheim, pleased that even in its truncated version *Foolish Wives* was a commercial success nonetheless accused Laemmle and Thalberg of releasing just 'the bare bones' of his story.

Considering all the problems that presented themselves during the shooting of *Foolish Wives* it was perhaps surprising that Universal took another chance with von Stroheim. Thalberg, though, was an astute young man who had the ability to recognize genius when he saw it. He was loathe to lose the services of a director of von Stroheim's quality so he said 'yes' when von Stroheim presented his next project, *Merry-Go-Round* the story of an impossible romance between an aristocrat and a girl of the people. Thalberg, however, was careful to take out insurance. When von Stroheim announced that he would once again like to play the villain in the new film Thalberg refused the request and told the director to hire another actor. During the shooting of *Foolish Wives* von Stroheim had protected himself by appearing in the film and shooting all the scenes in which he appeared first. That way, if there was any trouble, it would mean reshooting the entire picture.

Taking out insurance was just about all that Thalberg could do. Once shooting started he had to cross his fingers and hope that von Stroheim would behave. As he couldn't be on set every minute of the day he sent down a 'unit production manager' to check all the expenses and details of physical production. The man's name was James Winnard Hum. He kept a diary of the production. On one occasion he noted that if von Stroheim decided at the last minute that certain props were crucial he would hold up work until they could be located. Von Stroheim also showed frequent displeasure with the scenic department. When he saw that the grass on a bridle path was not the proper shade of green (the film he was shooting was obviously in black and white) he stormed around the set, cursing technical director Archie Hall as a 'son of a bitch'. 'Do you honestly think I'm going to shoot it?' he yelled.

Erich von Stroheim

During the five weeks that von Stroheim was involved with *Merry-Go-Round* there was a general air of disrespect for studio authorities most of it engendered by von Stroheim himself. He took his time, behaved temperamentally and when it came time for him to shoot an orgy scene indulged himself to the full. William Daniels, one of the cameramen on the film later remembered the scene only too well: 'He had all the extras playing Austrian officers *really* drunk; he served real champagne by the bucketful and whiskey as well; all the extras got loaded. A girl stepped naked out of a punch bowl. Stuff like that. I think it was during a shot where I irised in on her that von Stroheim passed out cold.'

When he was eventually fired from *Merry-Go-Round* von Stroheim was not unhappy to go. He had had enough of Thalberg and his constant bickering. The 24-year-old heir apparent irritated him and he disliked being under supervision. Things had been different when Laemmle had alone been in charge of the studio; since Thalberg's arrival he was unable to function properly. He would, he announced, find employment elsewhere.

There was some surprise when he joined The Goldwyn Company which had been formed in 1917 by Samuel Goldwyn (then Goldfish) and hardly rated as one of the major Hollywood studios. The big attraction for him was that there were no strings. He would be allowed to film all of the company's major productions with the minimum of interference. There would be no-one like Thalberg around to ruin his pictures. The epic *Ben-Hur* was one of the films that enticed von Stroheim to Goldwyn but as that was still some way in the future he interested himself instead in filming a book that had intrigued him for years and that he always dreamed of bringing to the screen.

The book was Frank Norris' *McTeague*. It's Zola-like realism made it the first naturalistic American novel and one that exercised a profound influence on Theodore Dreiser and other American realists. Its story was that of the slow decline, degradation and death of a San Francisco dentist and his wife, a woman whose obsession with gold turns her into a crazed miser and her husband into a drunkard and a murderer. It was hardly the stuff of which family entertainment was made but von Stroheim set about filming it as no film-maker had filmed a novel before. Retitling it *Greed* he shot it page for page, shooting on location in San Francisco streets (even those actually described in the novel) and eschewing all thoughts of filming on the Goldwyn backlot.

He even ventured into Death Valley (where Norris had set the climax to his book) to photograph the scenes in which two men die together shackled by the wrist in the blistering heat of the Mohave desert. Quite why he needed to do this when there was a suitable location on the dunes near Oxnard, a desert area not far from Los Angeles, can only be answered by the statement: 'It was a von Stroheim picture!' Valentino may have used the dunes to race across the sand in *The Sheik* but that did not impress von Stroheim. He said:

I insisted on Death Valley and Death Valley it was. There were no roads and no hotels. We were the only white men (41 men – one woman, a script girl) who had

'Hate each other as much as you both hate me!' Erich von Stroheim on location in Death Valley for Greed (1924).

penetrated into this lowest point on earth (below sea level) since the days of the pioneers. We worked in 142 degrees fahrenheit in the shade and *no* shade. The results I achieved through the heat and the physical stress were worth the trouble I had gone to. It would have been absolutely impossible to get anything near it in Oxnard.

According to the insurance company covering the expedition the hazards in Death Valley included not only the temperatures but also quicksands, poisonous reptiles and insects, air pockets of death-dealing gas and poisonous fumes, and waterholes that were poisoned with arsenic and brought instant death with just one drink!

Paul Ivano, a young French cameraman who had already shot some second-unit camera for American films, was called in by von Stroheim to shoot inserts of landscapes and sunrises. He was one of the crew who quickly wilted. He remembered:

I was roped in to handle an extra camera in Death Valley and like a fool I said, 'yes, I'll go'. Stroheim used to walk around in shorts, and gloves, and a colonial helmet, and I think he had a gun strapped on in case a rattlesnake came out. One of the cooks on the company died – I think he had high blood pressure and the heat didn't help. The paint on the cars curled up and fell off. You couldn't touch a piece of metal. And Stroheim seemed to like it. I could only stand it for about three and a half days.

Von Stroheim had deliberately sought out the worst part of Death Valley at the hottest time of year. For actors Gibson Gowland (who played the dentist, McTeague) and Jean Hersholt who featured as his mortal enemy, it was like

The final confrontation! Jean Hersholt and Gibson Gowland face to face in Death Valley (Greed, 1924).

living a nightmare. Hersholt remembered:

Every day Gibson Gowland and myself would crawl across those miles of sunbaked salt, the hunted murderer pursued by the man who had sworn vengeance on him. I swear that murder must have been in both our hearts as we crawled and gasped, bare to the waist, unshaven, blackened and blistering and bleeding, while Stroheim dragged every bit of realism out of us. The day that we staged our death fight I barely recollect at all. Stroheim had made our hot, tired brains grasp that this scene was to be the finish. The blisters on my body, instead of breaking outwards, had burst inward. The pain was intense. Gowland and I crawled over the crusted earth. I reached him, dragged him to his feet. With real blood-lust in our hearts we fought and rolled and slugged each other. Stroheim yelled at us, 'Fight, fight! Try to hate each other as you both hate me!'

During filming, *Greed* became the most talked about movie being made in the United States. In an interview in *The New York Times* von Stroheim explained his obsession with the documentary realism of his picture. He said:

The screen must be life's mirror, part of the time, anyway. It is possible to tell a great story in motion pictures in such a way that the spectator forgets he is looking at beauteous little Gertie Gefelta, the producer's pet, and discovers himself intensely interested, just as if he were looking out of a window at life itself. He will come to believe that what he is gazing at is real – a cameraman was present in the household and nobody knew it. They went on in their daily life with their joys, fun and tragedies, and the camera stole it all, holding it up afterward for all to see.

By the time he wrapped production, in October 1923, von Stroheim had shot 446,103 feet of negative and spent close to $750,000. Shooting had taken him 198 days. His 'final cut' ran 42 reels, a film of roughly 9 to $9\frac{1}{2}$ hours. Once again von Stroheim's plans were to show the film on two consecutive evenings. If he had moved just a little quicker during the editing stages he might have persuaded the Goldwyn company to accede to his wishes. But he was always a fussy editor and was unable to present his rough cut until January 1924.

One who saw it in its rough cut version was newspaperman Harry Carr. He wrote:

> I saw a wonderful picture the other day – that no-one else will ever see. It was the unslaughtered version of Erich von Stroheim's *Greed*. It was a magnificent piece of work, but it was 42 reels long. We went into the projection room at 10.30 in the morning; we staggered out at 8.00 that night. I can't imagine what they are going to do with it. It is like *Les Miserables*. Episodes come along that you think have no bearing on the story, then 12 or 14 reels later it hits you with a crash. For stark, terrible realism and marvellous artistry, it is the greatest picture I have ever seen. But I don't know what it will be like when it shrinks from 42 to 8·reels.

Von Stroheim didn't get his way with the Goldwyn studio. They suggested that he cut, and cut by quite a lot. This time, von Stroheim refused to let anyone else edit his work and laboured over the film himself. He worked for nothing as his contract only stated that he receive payment for direction. By March 1924 he had halved the picture, reducing it from the rough cut of 42 reels to 22. He told Goldwyn that that was as much as he could cut and that in his opinion the film was ready for showing.

Quite whether those at Goldwyn agreed is not certain but a month later it was all academic anyway. The Goldwyn company merged with Metro and Loews to form Metro-Goldwyn-Mayer and the decision was taken out of their hands. Von Stroheim, totally absorbed in his editing had failed to heed the warning signs of the merger and with it the fact that his new boss would be former junk tycoon Louis B. Mayer, an All-American with a liking for homely family entertainment, and – as his trusted young assistant – none other than Irving Thalberg.

Von Stroheim, distraught that he would once again be under the supervision of the young Thalberg, and remembering what Thalberg had done to *Foolish Wives*, sent a copy of the 22-reel *Greed* to Rex Ingram, long a friend of his. He asked him to see if there was anywhere he could make further cuts. Ingram judiciously pruned the film down to 18 reels and sent it back with a note to von Stroheim. It said: 'If you cut one more foot I'll never speak to you again.'

When they saw the 18-reel *Greed* neither Mayer nor Thalberg liked the film. Mayer referred to it as 'a vile epic of the sewer'. When von Stroheim, by now tired and depressed and realizing his film was slipping away from him, refused to cut another frame, they took it to the studio and turned it over to Joseph Farnham, one of their top title writers. Farnham prepared the 10-reel version that was eventually released. He hacked out huge chunks of action and attempted to fill the gaps with inept title cards. But there was no disguising the extent of the mutilation.

Von Stroheim later recalled his feelings at the time. He said:

> Mayer didn't give a damn about what Rex Ingram had said. He felt that the picture would be a total loss to the company anyway and that it must be cut to ten reels. It was given to a cutter at thirty dollars a week who had never read the book nor the script and on whose mind was nothing but a hat. The man ruined my work of two years. During those two years I had hocked my house, my car, my life insurance to be able to continue to work... At the time when the same company made slapstick and farce comedies of fourteen reels length, my picture was arbitrarily cut down to nine or ten. The rest of the negative was burned to get the forty three cents worth of silver out.

If von Stroheim hadn't needed the money its conceivable that his Hollywood career might have ended then and there. Ironically, the man who helped save it was Irving Thalberg who, although despairing of von Stroheim's lack of discipline held the director's talent in great esteem. He offered von Stroheim *The Merry Widow*, saying that he didn't care what he did with it, just as long as he retained two sequences – one in which the widow and the prince waltz at the Paris embassy and the one at Maxim's – since they would both be expected by the public who cherished the Franz Lehar operetta.

Von Stroheim turned the film into an orgiastic black comedy complete with sadism, perversion and debauchery, all of it taking place behind the bittersweet facade of Hapsburg society. But he was far from proud of it. He later said:

> When I saw how the censor multilated my picture *Greed* which I did really with my whole heart, I abandoned all my ideals to create real art pictures and made pictures to order from then on. My film *The Merry Widow* proved that this kind of picture was liked by the public, but I am far from being proud of it and I do not want to be identified at all with so-called box-office attractions. So I have quit realism entirely... When you ask me why I do such pictures I am not ashamed to tell you the true reason. Its only because I do not want my family to starve.

On *The Merry Widow* von Stroheim found himself having to work for the first time with established stars. Usually he liked to work with actors who were selected for their suitability for their roles not their star quality. On *The Merry Widow* he was saddled with Mae Murray and John Gilbert. After an initial skirmish Gilbert turned out to be easy to work with. Miss Murray did not. A star of jazzy comedies that required little acting but a lot of dancing she let it be known that she wasn't worried one way or the other about working with

Stroheim as she always played herself anyway. This didn't exactly endear her to von Stroheim who clashed frequently with her on set. He quickly became bored with her tantrums and was frequently heard to growl to his cameraman: 'I've had just about enough of this Murray girl. Don't expect me back in the morning.' Once, during a love scene between her and Gilbert he grew so weary of her efforts that he turned his back on the scene and said in a loud voice: 'Tell me when it's over.'

The last straw occurred during the filming of the waltz scene. Miss Murray became incensed when von Stroheim insisted on showing her how to perform the dance. She stamped her feet, threw down her peacock-feathered fan, and screamed, 'You Hun! You dirty filthy Hun!' The Hun decided that this might be a good time to leave the production and left the set. Thalberg was on holiday so Mayer, seeing the opportunity to fire von Stroheim once and for all, announced that a new director Monta Bell would be taking over. The next day he brought him to the set only to be greeted by hissing and booing from the extras (many of whom were von Stroheim's buddies) and also the technicians. When one of the extras threw a punch Mayer decided it was prudent to withdraw and reconsider his decision. He brought Murray and von Stroheim together, had them photographed walking arm in arm to the set, and production continued.

There were other von Stroheim pictures after *The Merry Widow* but not many and certainly none at MGM. Paramount took a chance with him on a film called *The Weddding March*, a massive two-part tale of a royal officer who is torn between the love of a cripple and the girl he is forced by parental decree to marry. Once again it was a case of excessive length and excessive cost. Paramount simply followed the example of other studios. They took Part Two away from him when he was still shooting and released a cut Part One as the entire film. Part Two, mutilated, was shown in Europe as *The Honeymoon*.

Queen Kelly, made as a vehicle for Gloria Swanson and in which she'd sunk some of her own money was never completed. Over $600,000 had been spent when Swanson (who had got along famously with von Stroheim for a while) realized that ten hours of film had been shot (ten hours that would eventually be reduced to 40 minutes) and they were still only a third of the way through the picture. That meant that there was still four months still to go. She finally gave up on the film when they came to shoot the picture's African sequences in which, as a former convent girl, she is reduced to running a dance hall. She said:

> As soon as I saw the first rushes of the African sequences I knew we were in trouble. They were rank and sordid and ugly. Mr von Stroheim's apocalyptic vision of hell on earth was full of material that would never pass the censors. Something was terribly terribly wrong. What was called a dance hall in the script had unmistakeably become a bordello, steaming and filthy, on the screen. In my first scenes in this African part my dying aunt is marrying me off to an old man. Erich von Stroheim has cast Tully Marshall in the part, and not content to have him old he had turned him into a leering, slobbering repulsive cripple. Mr Marshall was

Erich von Stroheim

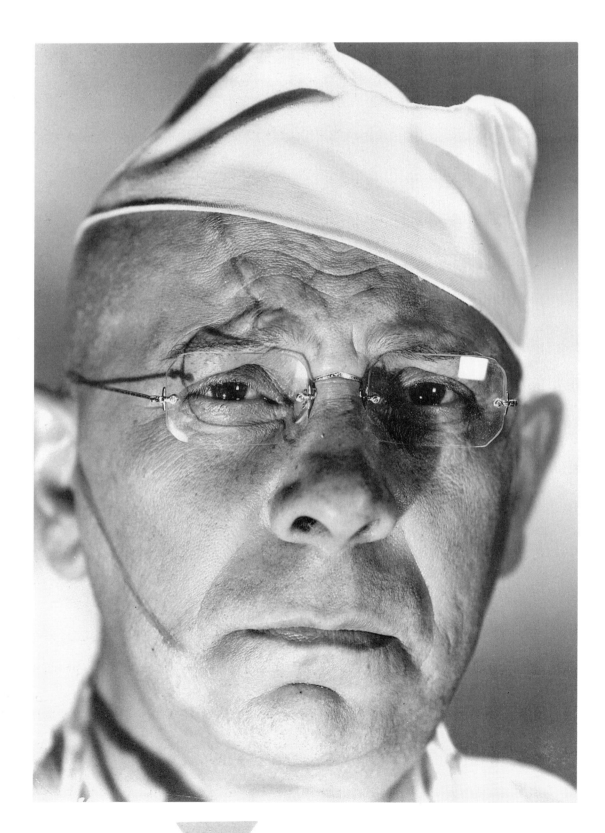

▶ *Von Stroheim! A great director reduced to B-movie status in Hollywood in the 1940s.*

playing the part to the hilt, as a sort of demented twitchy lecher in a greasy suit.
On my third day of shooting Mr von Stroheim began instructing Mr Marshall in
his own usual painstaking fashion, how to dribble tobacco juice onto my hand
while he was putting on the wedding ring. It was early morning. I had just eaten
breakfast and my stomach turned. I became nauseous and furious at the same time.

Gloria Swanson left the set, went straight to the nearest telephone and rang
Joseph J. Kennedy who was financing the production for United Artists. 'There's
a madman in charge here,' she said. 'He's shooting scenes that will never get past
the censor.'

Production shut down shortly afterwards. A reduced version of the film,
completed by Edmund Goulding, was shown subsequently in Europe. The picture
had a different ending and was never released in the USA.

It was twenty years before Swanson and von Stroheim worked together again.
Billy Wilder brought them together for his acid comment on Hollywood life,
Sunset Boulevard (1950). Swanson was brought out of retirement for the picture.
She played a once famous silent movie star who employs a young washed-up
screenwriter (played by William Holden) to write her comeback picture. Von
Stroheim played Swanson's butler/chauffeur and her former husband.

By then von Stroheim was no longer a film-maker. After the unfinished *Queen
Kelly* he directed two more films, both of them 1930s potboilers – *Walking Down
Broadway* which was re-shot by Alfred Werker and released as *Hello Sister*, and
The Emperor's Candlesticks. He returned to acting in whatever films became
available, first in Hollywood, then in Paris in the late 1930s and then in
Hollywood again during World War II when he was cast once again as Nazis and
militant Prussians. Apart from his prison camp commandant in Renoir's superb
La Grande Illusion few of his performances were memorable. Mostly they were
formula roles – spys, professors, generals, swindlers, night-club entertainers, even
on one occasion a fanatical film director. Billy Wilder was one of those who got
the best out of him when he cast him as Rommel in *Five Graves To Cairo*.
Wilder, long an admirer of von Stroheim's, was suitably in awe of the great man
at their first meeting. Said Wilder: 'It's an honour to be directing you Mr von
Stroheim. You were always ten years ahead of your time.' To which von
Stroheim replied: 'Twenty Mr Wilder, Twenty!'

Billy Wilder said:

He was fascinating; *le grand seigneur* at all times. There was something very odd and
yet noble and dignified about him. He wasn't a Von or anything like that, he had a
very heavy accent from the rougher suburbs of Vienna, but it didn't matter; he had
style.

He didn't resemble Rommel at all, but that didn't matter either: he gave the
audience the proper sense of illusion, a correct impression of the character. He
influenced me greatly as a director: I always think of my style as a curious cross
between Lubitsch and Stroheim. He was full of marvellous ideas. His makeup for
instance: it was black on the face and white on his head above the line of the cap –
you see, he pointed out that Rommel was always in the sun, and when he took his
cap off there would be no colour in the skin underneath.

He insisted on having two cameras slung around his neck. They had to be German; he even insisted on having film inside saying: 'The audience will sense if the films aren't inside; they'll feel they are merely props.' Of course, he later contributed ideas to *Sunset Boulevard* as well: the idea that the butler he played wrote all the fan mail for the lost star, Norma Desmond for instance. But then he would go too far. 'Let me do a scene', he said, 'where I'm washing and pressing my former wife Norma Desmond's panties. Please, I know I can do it.' And I said, 'Yes I know you can, but I don't want to shoot it.'

Billy Wilder found it wise not to discuss von Stroheim's silent pictures. He said: It would have taken him sixteen hours to explain the ten hours of *Greed*. He had a habit of rambling on forever if you started on one of his pictures. Mostly we talked about Vienna in the old days, about love and women. The obsession with foot fetishism, underwear fetishism, other sexual perversions which his pictures are filled with was the real Stroheim. He loved to go into detail about his own fetishes, and how he satisfied them. The movie he should have made was an adaptation of Krafft-Ebing's *Psychopathia Sexualis*. But he succeeded in slyly getting a lot of sex perversions into the films he shot in the 1920s. In regard to sex perversions Mr von Stroheim was not only twenty years ahead of his time, he was fifty years ahead of his time.

Ironically, Cecil B. De Mille, who had started in Hollywood at about the same time as von Stroheim was also in *Sunset Boulevard*. He played himself and was seen directing scenes from his epic *Samson And Delilah*. In 1950 everyone in the world knew the name of De Mille even though he was only half the director and half the artist von Stroheim had been at his peak. The name of von Stroheim had all but been forgotten.

Erich von Stroheim

▶ Erich von Stroheim à la cartoonist Vicky at the time of his 1955 visit to London's National Film Theatre.

Erich von Stroheim

Von Stroheim earned his one and only Oscar nomination (in the supporting actor category) for *Sunset Boulevard*. He didn't win. But then with his luck he almost certainly didn't expect to. Looking back, its doubtful whether he and Hollywood would have found a suitable marriage at any time, be it in the silent or the sound eras. Rebel and maverick directors never really succeeded in Hollywood. Witness the case of Orson Welles and, more recently, Michael Cimino with his *Heaven's Gate*.

Von Stroheim lived his final years in France. He died there in 1957, aged 71, shortly after being awarded the Legion of Honour. The award pleased him; it was one of the few he had ever received. And he enjoyed the atmosphere of France. When he was called on by the BBC to compose a eulogy for D.W. Griffith on the occasion of that great director's death, he said:

> If you live in France and you have written one good picture, or directed one outstanding film, fifty years ago and done nothing since, you are still recognized as an artist and honoured accordingly. People take off their hats and call you *maître*. They do not forget. In Hollywood you're as good as your last picture. If you didn't have one in production within the last three months you're forgotten, no matter what you had achieved before.

In the final analysis there seems to have been no way that von Stroheim could have ever succeeded in Hollywood. On the one hand he was a creative genius and that in itself was a big enough hurdle to overcome. He was also a profligate spendthrift and that too was against him. When the two were combined he became, in Hollywood parlance, a liability. The mutilation of *Greed* tarnished von Stroheim's career once and for all. He ended as one of the cinema's tragic figures, always searching for projects that never materialized. His was a career littered with great follies because he failed to meet Hollywood on its own terms. If just once he had been able to curb his excesses and compromise just a little... But then, if he had, he wouldn't have been von Stroheim.

10. Orson Welles

Orson Welles

◀ *Orson Welles in his mid-twenties, at the time of his first arrival in Hollywood.*

Hollywood never really took to Orson Welles. When he arrived there in June 1939 he knew nothing of the cinema and had never made a film in his life. He'd enjoyed success on Broadway where he'd staged, among others, an all-black *Macbeth*, and on radio he'd sent America into blind panic with his broadcast of *The War Of The Worlds*. But as far as the cinema was concerned he had absolutely no experience whatsoever. The struggling RKO studio (in 1939 just about to lose their money-making stars Astaire and Rogers) saw him as their salvation, offering him a contract that allowed him to make just about anything he liked.

What he made, of course, was the masterly *Citizen Kane*, a film that told, through the eyes of the people who knew him, the life and death of a newspaper tycoon. Welles used no stars, just his Mercury Company which he had brought with him to Hollywood – Joseph Cotten, Agnes Moorehead, Everett Sloane, Ray Collins. Yet he succeeded in making a film that many still consider the finest ever made in America, indeed anywhere. He was just 25 when he actually filmed *Kane* and 26 when he saw its release. Yet by then he was already on the way down. Orson Welles reached the top and began the downward slide at exactly the same moment. That moment occurred on 1 May 1941 when *Citizen Kane* premiered at the Palace in New York. Afterwards, despite all the critical acclaim, things fell apart.

They needn't have done if Welles had met Hollywood halfway and managed to get a couple of commercial successes under his belt early on. Then things might have been different and his stay in Hollywood might have stretched over many years. He might even have managed to film some of the projects he was still hoping to put before the cameras some forty years later. But that was never Welles' way. The commercial side of the cinema didn't interest him. He made films in his own highly individual style and with a technical virtuosity that no-one in Hollywood has quite been able to match since. He had no film training, he just used his instinct and (as he would subsequently gleefully remind people) his 'flawed genius'.

But he paid a price (as did film-lovers) for his refusal to compromise. Between 1941 and 1958 he directed just six films in Hollywood, a paltry output for a man acclaimed as one of the true geniuses of the American cinema.

Just before his death Welles, who was an accomplished magician as well as an actor/writer/director, said:

> I've always dreamed of being a popular entertainer and the only way I can do that is to use magic, which I love. I have to do magic on television because I've never had a friend who has asked me to do a trick. I once went to a birthday party for L.B. Mayer with a rabbit in my pocket but nobody asked me to do anything. The rabbit peed everywhere and I had to go home.

The story may be apocryphal but it indicates that Welles, although perfectly happy to entertain in cabaret, on television and on Broadway never thought of entertaining in a similar fashion in the film medium. And that, in the end, may

have been his Achilles heel. He seemed to equate commercial success with artistic failure and could never come to terms with the fact that artistry and the box-office could sometimes go hand in hand. For all his artistic genius he seemed forever naïve about the workings of the film capital. He enjoyed playing with his electric trainset but he had no idea of how to keep the wheels turning in his favour.

His troubles began a few weeks before the release of *Kane* when word reached William Randolph Hearst that the film was a caricature of his life. Gossip columnist Louella Parsons who worked for Hearst, first twigged it when she attended a private screening of the film early in 1941. She left in a fury before the end realizing she'd just seen a movie about the life of her boss. Like Kane, Hearst was a newspaper tycoon and in Welles' film the resemblance between the two men seemed to extend to even the smallest details. Susan Alexander, the singer in Kane's life, was said to correspond to Marion Davies, a starlet with whom Hearst had fallen in love and who had become his mistress. Also the name of 'Rosebud', used for Kane's boyhood sledge in the film, was supposedly the pet name used by Hearst for Miss Davies' pudenda, at least according to those who were on close acquaintance with the tycoon.

An incensed Hearst offered RKO $900,000 (the cost of the film) if they would burn the negative. He got nowhere. He could hardly come out openly and claim that the film was based on his life with Miss Davies because that would have given the relationship too much publicity. Instead he decided on a different ploy. He threatened the other studio moguls that he would reveal some of the juicier moments in their sex lives if they dared to show the film in their theatres. With Louella Parsons at the ready to provide the ammunition, Warners, Loews and Paramount, all of whom relied heavily on the Hearst papers for advertising outlets, backed off and refused to show the film.

RKO thus had difficulty in finding circuit bookings for *Kane*. Eventually they exhibited it solely in their own cinemas. In New York and Los Angeles independent cinemas had to be hired. Hearst, realizing he had RKO on the run, banned his papers, which spanned America, from mentioning any RKO film. With the odds so heavily stacked against it *Citizen Kane* flopped at the box office. The critics hailed it as a masterpiece but the public, although interested by all the advance publicity, weren't interested enough to sustain its momentum. The film grossed nearly $24,000 in its first week in New York but by the ninth week receipts were down to a dismal $7,000. RKO, desperate to salvage something out of the fiasco, resorted to the most basic advertising to sell the film. One slogan read: 'What made this cutie walk out on $60,000,000? A girl who never made more than $15 a week – wed to the world's wealthiest man! But neither she – nor any woman – could endure his kind of love!' Such advertising made no difference. *Citizen Kane* finished up in the red. Even at Oscar time it failed to garner any of the major awards. The only Oscar it received, despite nine nominations, was for best screenplay, the award being shared by the co-writers Welles and Herman J. Mankiewicz.

▲ *The world première of* Citizen Kane, *The Palace Theatre, New York, 1 May 1941.*

▶ *Master and mistress: Orson Welles and Dorothy Comingore in* Citizen Kane.

Orson Welles needed luck at this point in his career and he needed it far more than when he had first begun work on *Kane*. Then his cameraman Gregg Toland had told him that he could learn all he needed to know about shooting a film in just ten minutes. And by studying John Ford's *Stagecoach* more than forty times, and the German silent expressionist film *The Cabinet Of Dr Caligari* almost as frequently, Welles had proved that a director didn't need twenty years' training to be able to make a good picture.

His choice of his second film proved to be his undoing. He considered works

by Hemingway, Maugham, Mark Twain and others. Also a version of Charles Dickens' *The Pickwick Papers* with himself as Pickwick or, failing that, W.C. Fields. In addition he contemplated *A Life Of Christ* (photographed by Gregg Toland), a film of *Cyrano de Bergerac* and an account of the Landru murders, a story eventually filmed by Chaplin as *Monsieur Verdoux*.

Close friends advised him to think less ambitiously and to film something more straightforward. Welles may or may not have listened to such advice but he certainly failed to heed it. Instead, he chose to film Booth Tarkington's *The Magnificent Ambersons*, a sombre story of the decline of a wealthy Midwestern family at the turn of the century. As a novel it was superb, as the material for a film to be released in 1942 when America was in the early stages of fighting a war it was a disastrous choice. When completed it ran for 135 minutes and by all accounts was as exhilarating as *Kane*. Some said that it was an even superior film. But by the time the RKO studio had finished with it it had been cut to 89 minutes. If Welles had not been away in Brazil trying to put together the documentary *It's All True* he might have managed to save it. Instead, it was left to editors Mark Robson and Robert Wise to cut the picture. Wise tried to keep in touch with Welles by phone and act according to his instructions but Welles was difficult to reach, there were delays in communication and in any case the director seemed to be more interested in spending money and enjoying South American girls than he did in editing his film long distance. No doubt if he had known just what damage RKO would inflict on *Ambersons* he would have made more strenuous efforts to hold onto his picture but by the time he realized just how much harm had been done it was too late.

In the end, RKO shot a happy ending to the film, one that was totally out of keeping with everything that had gone before. Six months later all of the cut footage was discarded and used for the then precious silver in the film.

Very few people saw the full-length *The Magnificent Ambersons*. Those who did at previews were the lucky ones, although they certainly didn't think so at the time. Mark Robson said:

> Bob and I took the film out to preview, and I guess in one fell swoop about a quarter of the theatre audience got up and left. Then about five minutes later another quarter left, and then finally the last half of the audience left, until there were about two or three people remaining in the theatre and many angry patrons waiting for us outside.
>
> So we figured we had quite a lot to do. We took the picture back and continued re-editing it throughout maybe ten or fifteen previews. Towards the end Bob Wise and I were no longer looking at the film but at the audience, watching to see if any of them left. We'd say, 'Maybe this fellow's just going to the men's room.' And a little later, 'Oh, here he is, he's back.' Finally the picture was played so that nobody left the theatre. That is basically the film that is now called *The Magnificent Ambersons*.
>
> I must say that the original version was simply marvellous; it was truly The *Magnificent Ambersons*. Theatrically wonderful; photographed by Stanley Cortez superbly. But it was so advanced, so ahead of its time, that people just didn't understand it.

The Magnificent Ambersons brought to an end Welles' association with RKO. He'd also appeared in, but had not directed, the Eric Ambler thriller *Journey Into Fear* and been recalled from location on *It's All True*, which was abandoned because of the excessive cost. And that was it as far as RKO was concerned. Welles' enemies in Hollywood who had been taking careful note of his problems and enjoying every minute of his fall from grace wished for just one more thing – for him to leave Hollywood altogether. And if he'd headed back to the Broadway stage he doubtless would have been better off, for the stage had always been his first love and there were no movie moguls in New York City.

There was, however, a beautiful auburn-haired actress called Rita Hayworth in Hollywood and it was she, rather than any outstanding film offers, that kept him there after his break with RKO. He had first met her at a party given by Joseph Cotten in 1943 and later persuaded her to join the magic act that he and Cotten were presenting in a huge tent, just off Hollywood Boulevard, for the entertainment of servicemen. Welles sawed her in half a few times and then married her. The union, labelled by the press 'Beauty And The Brain', foreshadowed that of Arthur Miller and Marilyn Monroe a decade later. Louella Parsons was one of many who predicted it would not last. She did not give her blessing.

Rita Hayworth, who by her own admission, was not the most intellectual of girls, went into things optimistically when she said: 'I'm a dancer and dancers are not noted for their brains. I've been on the stage since I was twelve, with no time for books or learning but I intend to catch up on my reading.' The reading included Shakespeare, Shaw, Molière and Turgenev as Welles sought to 'improve her mind'. He also told her which classical records she should listen to and what art galleries and museums she should visit.

For his part Welles was only too happy to be enjoying the limelight once again, this time as one of the most famous husbands in Hollywood. He also delighted in his wife's beauty, proving that he had lost none of his flare for publicity. On one occasion he brought two photographers to her bedside in the dead of night, roused her suddenly and then, as she sat up startled, had her snapped with a photo-flash to prove that she looked lovely at any hour of the day or night.

The marriage, although not dissolved as quickly as some had predicted, was scarcely a contented one. Even the birth of a daughter, Rebecca, failed to make it work. Something else that didn't help was that Welles had been reduced to acting in films rather than directing them and Rita's career, which was then at its peak with musicals like *Cover Girl*, was putting the former *wunderkind* in the shade.

Welles played Rochester in *Jane Eyre*, a returning war veteran who has undergone plastic surgery in *Tomorrow Is Forever* and appeared as himself with Marlene Dietrich in a spoof of his magic act in *Follow The Boys*. None of which proved to be very satisfying. Even though he had a new radio show called *Orson Welles' Almanac* and wrote political columns for magazines there was no escaping the fact that he was fast becoming just another name in Hollywood. *Citizen Kane*

Hunted Nazi Franz Kindler (Orson Welles) in a scene from the Sam Spiegel production The Stranger, *directed by Welles in 1946.*

was four years behind him and already many felt that he would never again get the chance to direct. The moguls considered him to be a commerical risk and he could not rid himself of the label 'genius'. He said bitterly: 'A genius in the Hollywood dictionary is somebody who is either dead or unavailable.'

The offer to direct again came right out of the blue. It was made by an independent film maker named Sam Spiegel who was then making something of a name for himself in Hollywood. He agreed with the boss of International Pictures, William Goetz, to approach Welles about a thriller they were about to embark on called *The Stranger*. At first they thought of employing Welles only as an actor. Spiegel said:

> The story was about a high-up Nazi official who flees to the States via South America and Mexico when the war is on its last legs, and hides himself in a small Middle West university town. John Huston and Anthony Veiler worked on the script, the role of the ex-Nazi being perfectly suited for Orson.
>
> I approached Welles about it and, after he had read the script, he agreed to play the part. He went on to tell me that he liked the script so much and the subject intrigued him so strongly that he would very much like to direct it as well. This put me in a spot. I had Huston in mind at the time; so at first I told Orson, in as tactful way as I could, that this would not be possible. Later I changed my mind and asked Orson to direct as well as star in the picture. I never regretted it. Orson did a remarkable job.

Nonetheless Spiegel did impose conditions when he agreed to let Welles direct *The Stranger*. Welles could modify and rewrite the script as much as liked before shooting, but then he had to guarantee that not a thing would be changed once shooting had begun. Welles also had to guarantee to pay International out of his own pocket should he default, and would get paid the bulk of his salary only when the film was finished.

Welles must have found the terms demeaning but he was so eager to get back behind the cameras he would have said 'yes' to almost any terms. They were certainly far removed from those offered by RKO when they first lured Welles to Hollywood some six years earlier. Then the contract had stated that he would get paid $100,000 for his first film, and $125,000 for his second, plus percentages of the profits after RKO had made back their initial outlay. He could also produce, direct, write and appear in both pictures or in any single capacity if he so desired. But, inferior though the terms for *The Stranger* were, they were still preferable to those that lay just around the corner.

Some critics argue that *The Stranger* is the perfect reply to all those who contend that Welles could have worked efficiently within the Hollywood system. They say it is routine, thin and commonplace, all of which is a little unfair, for it contains some bravura sequences – notably its climax when Welles is speared to death by the sword of the figure of an avenging angel on the top of a clock tower. Welles himself tended to side with the critics of the film, complaining there was little if anything of him in it, and what there was had been cut – notably a long exciting prologue as the Nazi flees across South America. Welles also didn't get on with Edward G. Robinson who played the war Crimes

THE MOST DECEITFUL MAN A WOMAN EVER LOVED!

Edward G.
ROBINSON
Loretta
YOUNG
Orson
WELLES

IN

The Stranger

WITH PHILIP MERIVALE
RICHARD LONG · BILLY HOUSE

DIRECTED BY *Orson Welles*

Produced by S.P. EAGLE Story by VICTOR TRIVAS and DECLA DUNNING Screenplay by ANTHONY VEILLER

UNITED ARTISTS

▲ *Five years after* Citizen Kane *and Welles takes third billing in* The Stranger, *the film that briefly reinstated him as a Hollywood director.*

Commissioner who hunts the Nazi to Connecticut. Spiegel remembered that 'Robinson was occasionally difficult to handle.' Robinson himself tended to dismiss the picture: 'Welles seemed to have run out of genius while making the film. It was bloodless and so was I.'

The Stranger *was brought in under budget and filmed in 35 days. It was shot on the Goldwyn lot and boasted the highest set built in Hollywood since* Intolerance, *the clock tower, baroque and forbidding, rising to 124 feet. To everyone's surprise the film made a profit – the only one of Welles' Hollywood pictures to do so. The Welles-Spiegel relationship was a convivial one, and indeed Welles was more than glad to have Spiegel's company when he arrived at Spiegel's home one night after being thrown out of his house by Rita Hayworth for his infidelities. Spiegel recalled:*

One night, well after midnight, Orson knocked at the door of my house. He was carrying two suitcases and looked ghastly. He was really terribly upset. I was sympathetic but I was worried too. Orson asked if he could stay with me for a few days, and, of course, I agreed. But I wondered what kind of work we would get out of him. How would the break-up of his marriage affect the job in hand?

I was worried but I need not have been. We sat up all night talking, and Orson unburdened himself to me at great length. He was in a mood of the most acute depression when we finally left for the studio, and I had great misgivings. On the set however his personal problems were forgotten. He applied himself to his work with his usual painstaking brilliance, as if he hadn't a care in the world. But in the evenings his melancholia would return, and he would sit for hours just staring at the wall.

It wasn't long afterwards that Rita announced they were separating. Welles had given her more than ample cause with his extra-marital relationships but it nonetheless came as something of a shock to learn that she was actually leaving him, especially as he was up to his eyes in work at the time on a lavish Broadway production of *Around The World In 80 Days*. Welles was in charge of the direction, Mike Todd the production and Cole Porter the music. The show included everything from a full-stage circus with tumblers, wire-walkers and a magic show doing some violence to a crateful of ducks, geese and rabbits, to huge scenes featuring dozens of girls in beautiful expensive costumes and period crinolines. There was even a rumour that at one stage Welles auditioned an elephant. The whole extravaganza was to last but 75 days on Broadway and leave a gaping hole in Welles' pocket. Todd had run out of money while the show was still trying out in Boston. Welles was determined to keep the thing alive until New York and needed an urgent loan to raise the cash. In desperation he rang Harry Cohn, the tough talking boss of Columbia Pictures – his wife's studio. Orson Welles later recalled:

> I was stuck with a $40,000 costume bill and the play was in danger of being closed down if I didn't come up with the cash. I got Harry Cohn on the line and promised him a great picture that I would write, direct and star in if he would just wire me the $40,000 advance. Cohn kept asking me what the title was. I grabbed the book the cashier was reading called *The Lady From Shanghai*. The money arrived a few hours later.

The deal turned out to be one of the worst Harry Cohn ever made. It was not the $40,000 that worried him. It was the budget for the film that eventually transpired that gave him the nightmares. He had agreed to the film partly because Spiegel had told him that Welles was a reformed character and partly because he felt that a Welles/Hayworth picture would make an attractive box-office proposition. The fact that the pair were splitting up as man and wife provided him with extra publicity.

The budget for *The Lady From Shanghai* had originally been set at under a million dollars but it quickly soared to two million as things got out of control. Location shooting in Acapulco proved expensive, Welles' direction was clumsy and uninspired and the actors on the picture became uneasy as Welles rewrote on set the lines they had been learning just the night before. Welles also changed the look of Rita Hayworth. He cut her long auburn tresses and restyled her hair into a blonde bob. 'My God what has the bastard done?' screamed the Columbia bosses when they got a first glimpse at what Welles described as his new 'champagne blonde'.

According to the perenially bitchy Louella Parsons what Welles had done was to try and destroy his wife's image because he had realized that he was washed up as Rita's husband. All of which was nonsense but there was no escaping the fact that *The Lady From Shanghai* emerged as one of the most boring, confused and incomprehensible films of all time. The plot had something to do with an Irish sailor (Welles) who becomes involved with a beautiful woman and her lawyer husband and ends up a pawn in a murder. There are critics who wax lyrical about the film's bizarre qualities but those who yawn their way through the film's seemingly interminable 86 minutes are in the majority. Apart from a brilliantly filmed shoot-out in a hall of mirrors the film had almost nothing to recommend it. Harry Cohn was heard to mutter after viewing the film in the Columbia preview theatres: 'What the fucking hell was that all about?' No-one who had the misfortune to watch the film with him could give a satisfactory answer. The film was a box-office disaster. Welles called *The Lady From Shanghai*: 'An experiment – in what *not* to do.' It was released in 1948 a few months after his divorce from Rita. She described their break-up in just one sentence: 'I just couldn't stand his genius any more.' He, on the other hand went into some detail about why he was not a particularly good husband. As always, modesty was not the strongest of his virtues. He said:

> As a lover I'm the proverbial heel. Women all get tired of me sooner or later. I woo and make love with all the originality and enthusiasm I can muster up and everything goes fine. But women puzzle and frighten me. They always want to go on romancing when love has been won and all questions settled.
>
> Rita, for instance, is a beautiful girl, a lovely wife, a perfect mother. When we are together we have wonderful times and she is happy. But I have varied interests and I can't do anything about it. I could tell her that I'm going to change my ways, that I'll be home every night at a certain time. I would try conscientiously to live up to my promises and I might succeed for several months.
>
> But I would be acting, and a man gets tired of acting. A man can't change himself. I told Rita before we were married exactly what she would have to contend with, but I suppose, like every other girl, she thought she could change me.

The Lady From Shanghai was almost the end of Welles' Hollywood career. His last effort of the decade was a version of Shakespeare's *Macbeth*. The studio that offered him the facilities to make the picture (provided he could shoot it in 21 days at a maximum cost of $800,000 dollars) was Republic, a company that was just one step up from those that operated on Poverty Row. Welles' decline was complete. From *Citizen Kane* to a small budget version of Shakespeare at a studio that no-one in Hollywood had ever taken seriously amounted to total humiliation.

Orson Welles and Rita
Hayworth; pawn and *femme
fatale in the bizarre thriller*
The Lady From Shanghai,
*directed by Welles for
Columbia Pictures in 1948.*

Welles said he made *Macbeth* because he believed a good film could be made
cheaply and quickly and with the minimum of sets. Also the challenge appealed
to him. He tried to get Tallulah Bankhead for Lady Macbeth (which would have
taken a bit of swallowing) but she wouldn't agree to do the Scottish accent so he
chose Jeanette Nolan instead. Not surprisingly the end result was a trifle bizarre.
Welles sported some most unusual headgear in the title role and shadows and
dark camerawork hid the fact that the film had been made for next to nothing at

a breakneck pace. Welles often had two units working simultaneously on the set, rushing from one to the other with his directions and working late into the night to meet his deadline. He managed it even though he must have realized just how low he'd sunk. A 'B'-western was being filmed on the next set and John Wayne would drop in to watch the filming whenever he had the chance.

Welles' favourite story about filming *Macbeth* at Republic was when he required a large number of extras for a day. Welles said:

> They weren't exactly the most energetic of extras, nor the most keen. So I did two things. I had two cameramen dressed up as extras, with cameras, moving around among them. And then, when they had to charge the castle, which they were loathe to do because it required a little energy and moving, I shouted 'Lunch!' And what you see when everybody charges the castle is everybody running off to eat lunch. They were special Republic extras who hadn't been asked to do anything, you know, in forty years. 'Lunch!'

Welles said goodbye to Hollywood after *Macbeth*. There were few who worried too much about whether he stayed or went. The halcyon days of *Kane* were by then part of history even though the actual time span between *Kane* and *Macbeth* was only seven years. All the early promise had faded; Welles remained unbankable. At the age of 33 he had finished with Hollywood and Hollywood had finished with him – almost. In the late 1950s he did return briefly as an actor/director in a thriller called *Touch Of Evil*. Charlton Heston had been set to star and it was he who persuaded Universal, who were going to cast Welles in one of the leading roles, to allow Welles to direct as well. The result was a baroque film that showed that Welles had lost none of his virtuosity and flamboyance and could still use the cinema as well as anyone in the business. He even proved that he could still act on occasion without having to descend into ham. His corrupt sheriff Hank Quinlan who operates in a seedy Mexican town and matches wits with a narcotics cop is one of his best performances. It was difficult to believe however that when he directed and starred in the film he was only 43 years of age. Already his weight was well over twenty stone. As his guest star Marlene Dietrich says to him in the film: 'I didn't recognise you, you should have stayed off the candy bars.'

Apart from the occasional venture to Hollywood for an acting role Welles spent most of his final thirty-five years wandering round Europe. He didn't care what he did, just as long as he scraped together enough money to make the long cherished projects he knew he could never have made in Hollywood. Some he managed to complete – his award-winning *Othello*, his version of Kafka's *The Trial, Chimes At Midnight* in which he was superb as Falstaff. Others he started, left for a year or two, began again and then left again. *Don Quixote* was the most notable example remaining unfinished at the time of his death even though he had been working on it for some thirty years.

Welles found the money for all these ventures by embarking on just about everything that came to hand – on radio, TV and on film. He was memorable as

Orson Welles in costume as crooked cop Hank Quinlan, directing a sequence from Touch of Evil.

Harry Lime in Carol Reed's *The Third Man* but such roles were rare. Mostly his parts were commonplace, the kind of roles that any actor could have played, but not as colourfully as Welles who, to relieve the boredom as much as anything else, would ham his way through them all. Mongol emperors, tycoons, charlatans, cops, historical figures in tatty European epics – he would play them all just to stay solvent and plunge ahead with some future dream. Sometimes the films in which he appeared were so bad it seemed inconceivable that he could have agreed to appear in them.

In the end he was a sad, lonely figure. He was idolized by the younger generation of film-makers who would pay him homage at whatever European festival he was attending to try and raise the money for his next venture, and there was always something he was working on. In his final years it seemed as though he enjoyed the fight to get the money (and bitching about things when he didn't) as much as filming. His close friends said that he was afraid to finish something once he had started it and was nervous about being judged on a completed work, either because it might be a fiasco or perhaps with luck, another masterpiece.

But that was nothing new; he had always been that way. Apart from *Kane* he had usually become bored with a project three quarters of the way through. He left *Ambersons* to work on *It's All True*. If he'd have stayed he might have been able to prevent the ruthless hacking down of that picture. He complained about

▶ *Marlene Dietrich and Orson Welles enjoying a joke off set during the filming of the Universal International thriller* Touch of Evil *(1958).*

▼ *Joseph Cotten and Orson Welles, high up on the ferris wheel in Vienna in Carol Reed's* The Third Man *(1949).*

▶ *Orson Welles and Paul Newman in Martin Ritt's version of* The Long Hot Summer *(1958), adapted from the novel by William Faulkner.*

the editing that was done behind his back on such films as *The Lady From Shanghai, Macbeth* and *Touch Of Evil* but that seemed as though he was making excuses. It was *his* decision that he left the cutting to others and moved on to whatever project was occupying his thoughts. Somehow, he could never come to terms with the Hollywood system, either in the studio days or in the post-war years when a new set of moguls reigned. A TV producer said of him: 'Welles mastered the profession but not its games. His films were made on his terms or they simply weren't made.' Sam Spiegel remained an admirer to the very end. 'He never thanked me for saying it,' he said, 'but I always considered him the most underrated potentially commercial director in the whole world.'

John Huston, who used Welles as an actor on several of his films (*Moby Dick, The Roots Of Heaven, The Kremlin Letter*) and who featured in another of Welles' long list of unfinished pictures, *The Other Side Of The Wind*, said:

> Orson had a wholly undeserved reputation for extravagance and unreliability. Much of it dated from the time he went down to Rio de Janeiro for *It's All True*, got caught up in the drama and spectacle of the Mardi Gras and brought back a couple of hundred thousand feet that nobody knew what to do with. This single incident was absurdly over-publicized. I saw the way he worked. He was the most economical film-maker. Hollywood could well have afforded to have imitated some of his methods.

*Orson Welles as
SMERSH agent Le Chiffre in
the 007 spoof,* Casino
Royale, *1967.*

When I accepted an Academy Award for him it was for his contributions to
films over the years. It struck me that although he was being paid this tribute, not
one of the studios was offering him a picture to direct. Perhaps it was because they
feared him. People were afraid of Orson. People who hadn't his stamina, his force
or his talent. When they stood close to him, their own inadequacies showed up all
too clearly. They were afraid of being overwhelmed by him.

When he died, on 10 October 1985, Orson Welles was not an old man. A few
months earlier he had reached 70 but he had been in bad health for some years.
His weight was estimated at being 22 stone. He had a heart condition and suffered
from gout and diabetes. He'd always been a heavy drinker (although he was not
an alcoholic) and addicted to long fat cigars. In a determined effort to shed
weight he swam 20 lengths a day. It was to no avail. He was in his bed when he
died. A typewriter was on the table across his bed. A blank sheet of paper had
been inserted. He may have been thinking of his proposed film of *King Lear*
which he had been trying to get off the ground for many years and which looked
at last as though it would go before the cameras. At least, that's the way it
looked. With Welles, the whole venture would probably have been postponed for
another five years.

Although he often seemed bitter and sad, towards the end Welles would often
lighten his spirits (plus those who happened to be in his company at the time)
with endless Hollywood tales that were either true, partly true or just downright
lies. He told so many with so many variations that it's doubtful whether he knew
himself whether they were true or false.

He was always vastly entertaining about his so-called prodigious love life which
he assured people, had been grossly exaggerated. He said on one occasion: 'I was
no great lover. I'd love to write about all my failures as a Casanova, which are
sensational and very funny.' There was the time, for instance, when he first
attempted adultery and the romantic atmosphere was broken when, over the
hotel room radio, he heard himself as the famous voice of the Phantom asking the
familiar and all too relevant question: 'Who knows what evil lurks in the hearts
of men?' Or again when he met Marilyn Monroe at a party, took her upstairs
and started making love. A man who believed it was his wife who had gone
upstairs, banged on the door until it opened, punched Welles and then realized his
mistake.

As for Hollywood? He hated it – and it was ironic that he should die there
rather than in some Spanish villa or European hideaway. 'We live in a snake pit
here', he said. 'I've been keeping a secret from myself for forty years and that is
that I hate it. But I just don't allow myself to face that fact because it turns out to
be the only place to go.'

At the end of the day Orson Welles could and should have amounted to
something more than he did. He was too self indulgent and self-destructive and
too easily bored. Charlton Heston, a deep admirer of Welles, said: 'There was a
kind of maverick streak in Orson . . . he just wanted to work but, at the same
time, there was something in him that drove him to alienate the men with the

Orson Welles as himself in the 1973 production F for Fake.

money.' More than anything else Welles was an outsider and he preferred it that way. Flawed genius he might have been but his legacy was a remarkable one. Today, the younger generation remember him mainly for lager and wine advertisements on TV. Already though, those adverts are vanishing in the memory and in a year or two will be forgotten entirely. *Kane* and *Ambersons* and others will remain and be enjoyed anew. Said Jean Luc Godard:

> May we be accursed if we ever forget for one second that he alone, with D.W. Griffith – one in silent days, one in sound – was able to start up that marvellous little electric train. All of us always, will owe him everything.

Bibliography

BOJARSKI, R., *The Films of Bela Lugosi*, Citadel Press, 1980.

BOSWORTH, P., *Montgomery Clift*, Harcourt, Brace, Jovanovich, 1978.

BROSNAN, J., *The Horror People*, Macdonald's & Janes, 1976.

COTTEN, J., *Vanity Will Get You Somewhere: An Autobiography*, Columbus, 1987.

COWIE, P., *The Cinema of Orson Welles*, A.Z. Zwemmer, London/A.S. Barnes, New York, 1965.

ÇURTISS, T.Q., *Von Stroheim*, Farrar, Straus & Giroux, 1971

DMYTRYK, E., *It's a Hell of a Life But Not a Bad Living: A Hollywood Memoir*, Times Books, 1978.

FLYNN, E., *My Wicked, Wicked Ways*, Heinemann, 1960.

FORDIN, H., *The World of Entertainment: Hollywood's Greatest Musicals*, Avon Books, 1975.

FRANK, G., *Judy*, W.H. Allen, 1975.

GEIST, K.L., *Pictures Will Talk: The Life and Films of Joseph L. Mankiewicz*, Charles Scribner's Sons, 1978.

HAYDEN, S., *Wanderer*, Alfred A. Knopf, 1963.

HIGHAM, C., *Orson Welles: The Rise and Fall of an American Genius*, St. Martin's Press, 1985.

HIGHAM, C., *The Films of Orson Welles*, University of California Press, 1970.

HIGHAM, C. and GREENBERG, J., *The Celluloid Muse; Hollywood Directors Speak*, Angus & Robertson, 1969.

HUFF, T., *Charlie Chaplin*, Henry Schuman Inc., 1951.

HUSTON, J., *An Open Book*, Alfred A. Knopf, 1980.

JOHNSON, D. and LEVENTHAL, E., *The Letters of Nunnally Johnson*, Alfred A. Knopf, 1981.

KASS, J.M., *The Films of Montgomery Clift*, Citadel Press, 1979.

KAZAN, E., *A Life*, Alfred A. Knopf, 1988.

KOSZARSKI, R., *The Man You Love To Hate*, Oxford University Press, 1983.

LaGUARDIA, R., *Montgomery Clift: A Biography*, W.H. Allen, 1977.

LAMBERT, G., *On Cukor*, W.H. Allen, 1973.

LEAMING, B., *Orson Welles: A Biography*, Weidenfeld & Nicolson, 1985.

MASON, J., *Before I Forget*, Hamish Hamilton, 1981.

MINNELLI, V. (with HECTOR ARCE), *I Remember It Well*, Doubleday, 1974.

MORELLA, J.H. and EPSTEIN, E., *Judy: The Films & Career of Judy Garland*, Leslie Frewin, 1969.

NEGULESCO, J., *Things I Did and Things I Think I Did*, Linden Press/Simon & Shuster, 1984.

NIVEN, D., *The Moon's a Balloon*, Hamish Hamilton, 1971.

NIVEN, D., *Bring on the Empty Horses*, Hamish Hamilton, 1975.

NOBLE, P., *The Fabulous Orson Welles*, Hutchinson, 1956.

Bibliography

PARISH, J.R. and BOWERS, R. L., *The MGM Stock Company*, Arlington House, 1973.

RINGGOLD, G., *The Films of Rita Hayworth*, The Citadel Press, 1974.

ROBINSON, D., *Chaplin, His Life & Art*, Collins, 1985.

SANDERS, G., *Memoirs of a Professional Cad*, Putnam, 1960.

SCHARY, D., *Heyday*, Little Brown & Company, 1979.

SCHICKEL, R., *The Men Who Made the Movies*, Elm Tree Books, 1977.

SHIPMAN, D., *The Great Movie Stars: The Golden Years*, Hamlyn, 1970.

SHIPMAN, D., *The Great Movie Stars: The International Years*, Angus & Robertson, 1972.

SINCLAIR, A., *Spiegel: The Man Behind the Pictures*, Weidenfeld & Nicolson, 1987.

SPOTO, D., *Stanley Kramer: Film Maker*, Putnam, 1978.

STEMPEL, T., *Screenwriter: The Life and Times of Nunnally Johnson*, A.S. Barnes & Co. Inc./The Tantivy Press, 1980.

SWANSON, G., *Swanson On Swanson*, Michael Joseph, 1981.

TAYLOR, J.R., *Orson Welles*, Pavilion Books, 1986.

THOMAS, B., *Thalberg: Life and Legend of the Great Hollywood Producer*, Doubleday, 1969.

THOMAS, B., *King Cohn*, Barrie & Rockliff, 1967.

THOMAS, T., BEHLMER, R. and McCARTY, C., *The Films of Errol Flynn*, Citadel Press, 1969.

WALSH, R., *Each Man in his Time*, Farrar, Straus, Giroux, 1974.

WOOD, T., *The Bright Side of Billy Wilder, Primarily*, Doubleday, 1970.

ZOLOTOW, M., *Billy Wilder in Hollywood*, W.H. Allen, 1977.